In *Exposing the Devil's Playb* tactics of the enemy against the tactics of the enemy, how can we have victory? This kind of equipping and eye-opening revelation is extremely needed in the body of Christ today. John provides spiritual meat for readers so their eyes can open up to the spiritual realm and they, therefore, can have victory over the enemy. This is a powerful book that will help you grow to be a strong, victorious warrior of God.

—APOSTLE KATHRYN KRICK
PASTOR, FIVE-FOLD CHURCH
AUTHOR, *THE SECRET OF THE ANOINTING*

JOHN RAMIREZ

EXPOSING
THE DEVIL'S
PLAYBOOK

CHARISMA
HOUSE

For more resources like this, visit MyCharismaShop.com and the author's website at https://johnramirez.org.

Cataloging-in-Publication Data is on file with the Library of Congress.
International Standard Book Number: 978-1-63641-377-8
E-book ISBN: 978-1-63641-378-5

1 2024
Printed in the United States of America

Most Charisma Media products are available at special quantity discounts for bulk purchase for sales promotions, premiums, fundraising, and educational needs. For details, call us at (407) 333-0600 or visit our website at www.charismamedia.com.

DEDICATION

I DEDICATE THIS BOOK to my mother, Esther Martinez. She is the hero of my story in the natural, and King Jesus is the hero of my story in the supernatural. As I was growing up in the projects, I saw my mom endure hardship of all kinds through the hands of my alcoholic father—the physical beatings, emotional distress, psychologically fragmented mind, spiritually inundated-in-witchcraft practices of altars, statues, so-called saints, and demonic spiritual gatherings from time to time. My mom practiced these things out of ignorance, hoping she could see the light of day and escape the reality, the torment, and the bad seasons of her life. But my mom always smiled, always dressed up, had us ready for school, and had food on the table. She was my mom and my dad at the same time. With food stamps, government cheese, and school lunches, we managed to get by.

I love my mom, and I'm so proud of her. I remember when my father got shot and killed that rainy night when I was only thirteen years old and we stood in front of the gate of the social club, only a door separating us from my father's body. I saw my mom climb out of that. Even today, with my father no longer here, I see my mom enduring another season. My brother Jimmy, who was the closest to my mom, passed on unexpectedly. Sometime later my precious sister Desiree passed on. She was adopted from foster care as a baby—the same way we have been adopted as children of God from the foster care of the world by the Father through Jesus Christ—but she was truly my sister. I saw my mom overcome those losses with the help of Jesus Christ.

One Mother's Day, my mom and my brother went out to a restaurant to celebrate, and my mom had an allergic reaction to seafood. She was rushed to the hospital and almost died five times that one day. But what the devil meant for evil, God turned around for good. My mom had been a Jehovah's Witness for eight years, but none of the Jehovah's Witnesses showed up at the hospital to pray for her. I was a young Christian at the time, and all my Christian friends, including the pastor from my church, bombarded the hospital and prayed for my mom. That day my mom received the free gift of salvation, left the Kingdom Hall of the occult called Jehovah's Witnesses, and walked into the marvelous life of faith by becoming a follower of King Jesus.

I've seen the hand of God bless my mom in so many ways. At the age of seventy-seven my mom still sees Jesus in every area of her life, even as she goes through the most horrific chemo treatment a body can endure. My mom is my hero because she knows how to stand in the face of the devil, look him in the eye, and let him know, "Jesus Christ is my Lord and my Savior, and I will keep going on until He calls me home. No weapon formed against me will prosper." (See Isaiah 54:17.) I believe my mom, after all is said and done, is going to make Jesus Christ proud.

I'm proud of my mom, and I honor her, dedicating this amazing book to who she is, not only as my mom and my hero but also as a woman who stood in the face of adversity in every season of her life. I never hear my mom complain and say, "Why me?" She just smiles and believes that the sun will come out the next day.

I love you, Mom. You're the hero of my story, and I honor you yesterday, today, and tomorrow, in the mighty name of Jesus Christ our Lord and Savior. Amen.

—JOHN RAMIREZ

CONTENTS

This is my story. This is how I live—for
my Lord and Savior Jesus Christ.

But none of these things move me; nor do I count my
life dear to myself, so that I may finish my race with
joy, and the ministry which I received from the Lord
Jesus, to testify to the gospel of the grace of God.
—Acts 20:24, NKJV

AN EVANGELISTIC MESSAGE TO THE WORLD

I WANT TO SHARE some of my thoughts with you today as I write this amazing book. God called me to be an evangelist before He called me to minister deliverance, so I want to share with you the heart of an evangelist and why heaven is not only my home but yours as well. I hope my thoughts minister to you and touch your heart, showing you how much Jesus Christ loves you. One of my favorite scriptures is John 3:16: "For God so loved the world that he gave his one and only Son, that whoever believes in him shall not perish but have eternal life."

Love is an action word. God proved it through His Son, Jesus Christ. He paved the road back to heaven for you. It might be a road filled with rocks, bumps, potholes, turns, and all kinds of unexpected climate changes—but not global warming, which is a lie from the pit of hell. The road that you're on has signs that say One Way, Do Not Enter, Construction Ahead, Bridge Is Out, Danger, and Two-Way Street. These are a few of the signs of life when we're on this road.

HEAVEN IS MY HOME

Let me hit the rewind button and take you on an adventure. It might sound humorous, or it might sound like a fairy tale, but I believe there is truth behind every humorous story and every fairy tale, just like the horrific, demonic, and despicable movies and TV shows have truth behind their stories. I'm not going to get the popcorn and have a seat, but I'll tell you my story, and I would say this is your story too.

I believe we were created in heaven but born on the earth. I like to think I was sitting at home in a mansion in heaven one day, and an angel came and knocked on my door.

The angel asked, "John, are you ready?"

I said, "Ready for what?"

He said, "For this amazing adventure that the Lord and Savior created you for."

I stared at the angel perplexed and dumbfounded, and I asked him, "What adventure?"

He said, "It's called your birthday. Your name was picked out of the hat, and you're being sent to represent a kingdom that cannot be shaken or moved."

I looked at the angel and asked, "Me? Why me? Why not Fred next door? Or Julio down the block? Why is it my turn?"

The angel looked at me with no response, shrugged his shoulders, spread his wings, and said, "I simply don't know. The only thing I can say is God trusts you to go on this journey and get back home one day."

I packed up my bags and was on my way. I was given a birthday and sent into time to this thing called life. I started my way through the birth canal of a mother named Esther Martinez, was born on the earth in 1963 in Puerto Rico, and immigrated to the Bronx at the age of one. I wasn't given an instruction book or blueprint for how to get back home; I was just given parents and siblings and sent on my way.

I knew a piece of my heart was missing, but I didn't understand why. We are all born that way. We try to fit other pieces into that place in our hearts like trying to put together a puzzle, but the other pieces never fit. They were never designed to fit because that missing piece can only be filled one way.

I grew up in poverty in the projects of the South Bronx. I was initiated into witchcraft, thinking that I would find Jesus Christ there because the world and every religion has a form of godliness but denies the power (2 Tim. 3:5). I kept marching through life—the seasons, months, and years—as you are doing today. But as we march, we are always wondering in the back of our minds, When will we find the missing pieces that fit in our hearts?

The funny thing is that somewhere, somehow, through tragedies, certain events, and life's circumstances our minds always reflect on one thing: God in heaven. No matter what we face as we walk through life, we'll never reach our destination on this earth. Wherever we are geographically, spiritually, emotionally, and mentally, we know there is always something missing, but we can't put our finger on it. I want to show you the keys that will help you get back home to heaven where you really belong.

One of the first things they teach you in school is the alphabet, and the first three letters are *A*, *B*, and *C*. And just as those letters are the keys to the whole alphabet, they are also the keys to unlocking your heart and putting the right puzzle piece in there so you can complete the mission called life from the day you are born until the day you pass on and close your eyes for the last time.

Times Square Church is my favorite church in the whole world. Thank God for David Wilkerson, the founding pastor, who heard from God and was bold enough to plant a church in the crossroads of the world, New York City. He blessed my life and mentored me for a period of time as I walked him back and forth to church and other locations many times.

Today the senior pastor of Times Square Church is Tim Dilena.

He is one of my favorite pastors in the whole world. He knows the ABCs, and he repeats them every Sunday. You may wonder why he is stuck on A, B, and C. It's like the angels in heaven who are stuck on one lyric: "Holy, holy, holy, Lord God Almighty, who was and is and is to come!" (Rev. 4:8, NKJV). They don't continue from there; they cannot get past that as they stand at the throne of the magnificent God, King Jesus, the Savior of the world.

Tim Dilena talks about the ABCs every Sunday because A, B, and C represent the simple things we need to do to get back home to heaven:

- Accept
- Believe
- Confess

Accept Jesus as your Lord and Savior. Believe that He died on the cross. Confess your shortcomings and your sins. Follow the ABCs, and you're on your way to heaven.

The Bible says Jesus came from heaven to earth to die on the cross. He was buried, rose again in three days, and went back to heaven. I'm going to follow Him because He knows His way back home. I don't need a GPS. I don't need other religions because they don't know the way back to heaven.

I know my way back to my physical home. I don't need anyone to walk me. I don't need someone to tell me how to get there because I know how to get there. You can't get somewhere unless you know where it is. Jesus Christ knows the way back to heaven, so I'm going on His bus. It's all mapped out in three letters: A, B, C. How cool is that!

I believe my house in heaven is on the corner of Hallelujah Boulevard, right across the street from Paul the apostle. LOL!

The piece of the puzzle that will fill the missing place in your heart is Jesus, the Son of the Living God. He is the way, the truth, and the life (John 14:6).

I hope you receive Jesus. Allow Him to come into your heart, and give Him the pen so He can write your story. Let Him write your purpose and your destiny. You will have no regrets; I know because I don't have any regrets in my life. I left the world behind, and I am following the One who created me, gave me a birthday, and sent me into time. He's going to make a way for me to get back home one day. Mission accomplished.

I am an ambassador for the kingdom that will not be moved or shaken. You, too, can be part of the story if you say yes to Jesus Christ by following the ABCs: accept, believe, and confess. As soon as you do those things, find yourself a Bible-believing church, and you will be on the right path to succeed in a life that only God, the Lord Jesus Christ, can write. Amen.

—EVANGELIST JOHN RAMIREZ

THE PURPOSE OF THIS BOOK

I LOVE THE LORD's Prayer. It's powerful, and it brings so much comfort, healing, and truth to our lives.

> Our Father in heaven, hallowed be Your name. Your kingdom come. Your will be done on earth as it is in heaven. Give us this day our daily bread. And forgive us our debts, as we forgive our debtors. And do not lead us into temptation, but deliver us from the evil one. For Yours is the kingdom and the power and the glory forever. Amen.
>
> —MATTHEW 6:9–13, NKJV

This is the masterpiece of all masterpiece prayers. I once heard this story about it: Two guys were walking together. One told the other, "If you're so religious, let's hear you quote the Lord's Prayer. I bet you ten dollars that you can't do it."

The friend turned around and said, "You've got yourself a bet," and he started quoting: "Now I lay me down to sleep. I pray the Lord my soul to keep. If I die before I wake, I pray the Lord my soul to take."

His friend turned around, looked at him, and said, "Wow. I didn't think you had it in you." He then pulled ten dollars out of his pocket and gave it to his friend.

That is the spiritual condition of the church today. We think we know. We hope we know. But do we really know the spiritual warfare that we face and the spiritual warfare that is ahead of us?

I want to share my heart with you about the purpose of this book. I am writing it to help my precious brothers and sisters around the world to fight the good fight of faith and to remind them that our adversary, the devil, is not only a defeated loser and a defeated foe, but he is also under our feet at all times, looking up toward us as we walk on our journeys to fulfilling our purposes and our destinies. I'm going to prove that to you in the pages of this book.

By the grace of our Lord Jesus Christ, the Holy Spirit has given me the opportunity to put on paper the enemy's lies, deceptions, schemes, wiles, and methods of entrapment, along with his favorite weapons, which are hindrances, delays, blockages, and temptations. These will be exposed like never before, and you will see how much victory we have because the Bible, the Word of God, and Jesus Christ do not lie. This book contains teachable moments and spiritual nuggets that I want to share with the body of Christ to disciple and mentor people as they learn how to fight the good fight of faith.

Romans 8:35–39 says:

> Who shall separate us from the love of Christ? Shall trouble or hardship or persecution or famine or nakedness or danger or sword? As it is written: "For your sake we face death all day long; we are considered as sheep to be slaughtered." No, in all these things we are more than conquerors through him who loved us. For I am convinced that neither death nor life, neither angels nor demons, neither the present nor the future, nor any powers, neither height nor depth, nor anything else in all creation, will be able to separate us from the love of God that is in Christ Jesus our Lord.

Deuteronomy 28:13 tells us, "The LORD will make you the head, not the tail. If you pay attention to the commands of the LORD your God that I give you this day and carefully follow them, you will always be at the top, never at the bottom."

You and I were born in this time, in this season, in this moment of life to do what our King Jesus called us to do. I'm not talking about the President of the United States, Congress, or the Senate; they are often pawns in the devil's chess game. I'm talking about the King of all kings and the Lord of all lords—Jesus Christ. We will fight, and we will win. We will make Jesus proud that He picked us.

I highly recommend that you use this incredible book as a teaching tool to enhance your faith, to build yourself up in the faith and in the tactics of spiritual warfare so you can see the devil in your blind spot, and to help you spiritually understand the demonic strategies of the kingdom of darkness. That is what this book is about. I highly recommend that you combine it with my book *Fire Prayers* so you can hit the devil from both sides. As an add-on to the spiritual warfare fight I highly recommend *Prison Break* by Pastor Juan Martinez, a book for such a time as this. It is a blessing to the body of Christ.

Chapter 1

THE GREATEST WAR EVER

T HERE IS AN amazing story found in the Scriptures in the Book of Exodus. It's time that we believers have an exodus experience of our own with the Lord Jesus Christ and shame the devil and his demonic kingdom once and for all.

The greatest showdown that I can think of happened in Exodus 7. The story is powerful and anointed, and it shows God displaying His majesty and His power at its best. Let the Holy Spirit use this story to teach you, equip you, and set you free once and for all. When you read the account of the showdown, you will see the battle right in front of your eyes.

On one side of the showdown we have the devil, we have Pharaoh, and we have Pharaoh's magicians. On the other side we have God, we have Moses, and we have Aaron. Listen carefully because I want you to catch this in your spirit: Moses was eighty years old at this time, and his only weapon was a rod. His brother, Aaron, was eighty-three. At their age they could have been collecting Social Security, but they were working for the kingdom. How awesome is that?

THE ULTIMATE SHOWDOWN

This was the ultimate showdown: the devil and his team versus God and His team. Spiritually the point of the story is to show

1

how the devil entraps believers and brings hindrance, delay, and blockages into their lives. Through this powerful teaching on spiritual warfare, I want to show you how you can overcome the fiery darts of the enemy and stop his mind games today.

Rounds 1 and 2

> So Moses and Aaron came to Pharaoh, and so they did, just as the LORD had commanded; and Aaron threw his staff down before Pharaoh and his servants, and it turned into a serpent. Then Pharaoh also called for the wise men and the sorcerers, and they too, the soothsayer priests of Egypt, did the same with their secret arts.
>
> —EXODUS 7:10–11, NASB

Check this out. The spiritual warfare is on. God won one round, and the devil won one round. This is how the devil tries to captivate your mind, your thoughts, and your thinking, because you see God won one round and then the devil won one round. The enemy is playing tricks by putting doubt and question marks in your mind.

Rounds 3 and 4

> So Moses and Aaron did just as the LORD had commanded. And he lifted up the staff and struck the water that was in the Nile in the sight of Pharaoh and in the sight of his servants; and all the water that was in the Nile was turned into blood. Then the fish that were in the Nile died, and the Nile stank, so that the Egyptians could not drink water from the Nile. And the blood was through all the land of Egypt. But the soothsayer priests of Egypt did the same

> with their secret arts; and Pharaoh's heart was hardened, and he did not listen to them, just as the LORD had said.
>
> —EXODUS 7:20–22, NASB

God won a second round, and then the devil won a second round. Now the fight was even. This is one of the enemy's tactics in spiritual warfare; he wants you to believe he has the power to go toe to toe with God. This is when the believer cracks in his mind, his thoughts, his words, and his faith. This is when you start to believe in your subconscious, in your soulish realm, that the devil has the same power as God.

Rounds 5 and 6

> Then the LORD said to Moses, "Say to Aaron, 'Extend your hand with your staff over the rivers, over the streams, and over the pools, and make frogs come up on the land of Egypt.'" So Aaron extended his hand over the waters of Egypt, and the frogs came up and covered the land of Egypt. However, the soothsayer priests did the same with their secret arts, making frogs come up on the land of Egypt.
>
> —EXODUS 8:5–7, NASB

Now you see the witches trying to mimic our Lord. When we go through these kinds of trials and difficult moments, we can miss God's best. We miss God's moments on the battlefield because we're thinking to ourselves, "How could the devil win three rounds?" But the voice you are hearing is not your voice. It's the voice of the enemy, who has already made himself comfortable in your mind. We put question marks on God and on the battle. Again we ask ourselves, "How can the devil win three rounds and God win three rounds?"

Now our faith has dwindled, our fire has diminished, and we experience doubt, fear, and unbelief. These are weapons of the devil. The enemy capitalizes on your doubt, fear, and unbelief and gains leverage in the spiritual warfare battle in your life by bringing hindrances, delays, and blockages.

Know this: God allows the devil to go so far in order that He can teach us how to trust Him deeply and fully, how to believe Him completely, how to trust Him with everything we have in our spirits, and how to walk in true faith.

Round 7

> Then the LORD said to Moses, "Say to Aaron, 'Extend your staff and strike the dust of the earth, so that it may turn into gnats through all the land of Egypt.'" They did so; and Aaron extended his hand with his staff and struck the dust of the earth, and there were gnats on every person and animal. All the dust of the earth turned into gnats through all the land of Egypt. The soothsayer priests tried with their secret arts to produce gnats, but they could not; so there were gnats on every person and animal. Then the soothsayer priests said to Pharaoh, "This is the finger of God." But Pharaoh's heart was hardened, and he did not listen to them, just as the LORD had said.
>
> —EXODUS 8:16–19, NASB

My precious brothers and sisters, it's not what you hear with your natural ears that is important but what you hear with your spiritual ears, so listen to this carefully: God displays His majesty. He is all-powerful. He can take nothing and turn it into something. He can take the dust of the earth and turn it into gnats. He can take nothing and put DNA and a respiratory system in it. He can put a body on it. He can put eyes on it. He can put antennas on it and turn it into something.

When God took the dust of the earth and turned it into gnats that covered every person and animal in Egypt, He shamed the devil. He shamed Pharaoh. He shamed the magicians. That is why we can't be so quick to give in, give up, and surrender to the enemy. Romans 4:17 calls God "the God who gives life to the dead and calls into being things that were not."

Devil, how do you like them apples? We serve an awesome God.

Pharaoh learned the hard way that no one can beat God, because God showed up and showed off. The devil understands this too. You can't mess with God, and He proves it over and over again by showing up and showing off. The only way the devil can win is through you and me, by putting us in spiritual confinement, with spiritual limitations and restrictions. That brings fear, doubt, and unbelief into the battle.

You have the potential to be a great white shark; stop walking around like you're just a goldfish. If you're serving the Lord Jesus Christ, the devil wants you to serve Him only in freedom with restrictions. When we give in to the devil, we become mediocre Christians and live mediocre Christian lives. In other words, we worship in shackles. We read the Bible in shackles. We go to church in shackles. We praise God in shackles. We walk out our Christian lives in shackles. We have freedom but with restrictions as we allow the enemy to spiritually incarcerate us.

Isaiah 52:2 says, "Shake yourself from the dust, arise....Loose yourself from the bonds of your neck" (NKJV). Jesus died so you could walk in freedom with no restrictions. So stop living in shackles. Get up! Shake off the dust, remove the shackles the

5

enemy put on you—Jesus already unlocked them—and walk in faith and freedom, not in doubt and bondage.

Notice what happened to Moses and Aaron in Exodus 8:25: "Then Pharaoh summoned Moses and Aaron and said, 'Go, sacrifice to your God here in the land.'" The devil, through the mouth of his servant Pharaoh, told Moses and his people the same thing he is telling the people of the church today: "You can go to church and worship God, but don't go too far. I want you to stay in Egypt." In other words, the enemy wants us to stay in our current spiritual condition, with restrictions, and boundaries, confined by the box he tries to put us in.

Here in America, when we see something that looks like it can't be fixed we often legalize it instead of trying to find a tough solution for a tough problem. Many Christians do the same thing spiritually when they are faced with tough issues. Instead of having faith and breaking free from their shackles through the power of the Holy Spirit, they don't trust that God can set them free. They make excuses instead. They say, "I was born this way," "It runs in my family," "It's generational," "I'm a work in progress," or "I'm waiting on God." They keep the shackles on, and with their words they give the devil the legal right to continue to keep them bound. They give the devil power over their lives instead of giving the power to our Lord Jesus Christ.

The devil wants to confine you and put you in a place where he can control you. He wants to put boundaries on you to keep you from growing into the man of God or the woman of God that God has called you to be.

I think the Book of Numbers is one of the saddest books of the Bible. To paraphrase, a church of three million people started in one place geographically, and they were still in the same place forty years later. They were stuck inside boundaries God never intended for them to live within because they gave in to doubt, fear, and unbelief rather than trusting fully in God, who had already proven time and time again that He could take care of any obstacle they faced.

The Israelites grew old, but they never grew up. Many believers today, many brothers and sisters whom I love with all my heart, grow old in their walks but don't grow up spiritually.

Do you have courage? Do you have the faith to step out of the boat like Peter did? Do you trust God to break the shackles off you today? If so, repeat these prayers with me so God can set you free. By praying these prayers you let the devil know, "I refuse to stay in Egypt." Get ready, open your mouth, speak loud and clear, and let the devil know you are coming. It's time for war.

PRAYERS THAT WILL ASSASSINATE THE ENEMY

- *I confess that I am a child of God.*

- *I declare that I'm born again by the finished work of the cross of Jesus Christ.*

- *I am the head and not the tail, in the name of Jesus.*

- *Devil, today and tomorrow and forever I'm reigning with Christ, seated in the heavenly places.*

- *Satan, listen to me. My body is the temple of the Holy Spirit, in the name of Jesus.*

- *Today my life is hidden in Christ that I should live and not die. I will declare the works of the Lord forever, in Jesus' mighty name.*

- *Today I will see the goodness of the Lord upon my life, my family, my ministry, my purpose, and my destiny in the land of the living.*

- *My authority and my identity live in Christ Jesus, my Lord and my Savior.*

- *I confess I have been made to overcome, triumph, and win every fight, every battle, and every war in Christ Jesus, my King, my Lord, and my Savior. Amen.*

- *Yesterday, today, and tomorrow no weapon formed against me will prosper. Every demonic war, battle, and fight, and every tongue that speaks against my purpose, my destiny, and my season will be burned by the fire of the Holy Spirit, in Jesus' unmatchable name. Amen.*

Chapter 2

HIT THE REWIND BUTTON AND REMEMBER THE GOODNESS OF THE LORD IN THE BATTLE

AT TIMES I find myself spiritually perplexed and super surprised. I don't know if they call it crazy or mad. We're living in an era, a generation, and a season in Christianity when believers grieve the Holy Spirit in an astonishing way.

How easily we forget God's goodness. How easily we forget His signs, miracles, and wonders in the body of Christ and His great mercy and love for us. I know this chapter will help many of you refocus and hit the rewind button in your spiritual walk with the Lord Jesus Christ.

It's not that we grieve the Holy Spirit on purpose or do it with bad intentions, but we allow the devil to plague our minds and bring what I call spiritual dementia into our lives. It's time to hit the rewind button and see His goodness, His mercy, and His grace.

My Testimony 2023

I love the word *testimony* because it's not about me. It's not a humanity thing. It's a divine thing. I believe that when a believer says *testimony* it's like saying *Jesus Christ* because Jesus Christ is our testimony of the things that we go through, and He brings us to the other side. It's always about Him. It's never about us.

Before I share the story of my journey and my testimony from 2023, I need to share some things that happened earlier. In 1999 I had my second birth; I was born into Christianity. I remember it like it was yesterday.

I was connected to the world of demons, mediums, and the devil himself. They came after me to kill, steal, and destroy. I was rocked like I never would have imagined. I was tortured and tormented spiritually beyond human comprehension. I was dragged off my bed and choked in the middle of the night, my blood running cold and my hairs standing up on end. The room was pitch-black and ice-cold. I heard the footsteps of demons out in the hallway, and they came into my room and tormented me all night. I was even fighting to keep my soul in my body because the demons were ripping me apart, trying to remove my soul so I could be pronounced dead in my bed in the Bronx.

Still a baby Christian, I held on with mediocre prayers and fought off those demons and the devil himself every night until it stopped once and for all. But that was just baby stuff compared to what I went through in 2023. It was the hardest year of my Christian walk.

On one hand, I was ministering, seeing people set free and healed, and seeing demons being destroyed by the power of the Holy Spirit. I witnessed curses and witchcraft being uprooted out of people's lives. I saw signs, miracles, and wonders at practically every altar call. I even received the precious, priceless blessing of doctorate and bachelor's degrees and ordination papers from Dr. Douglas Wingate and Dr. Susan Wingate at Life Christian University.

Meanwhile, on the other side of the spectrum the devil and his cronies were launching the most horrific, tormenting demonic spiritual attack. There were days I couldn't breathe. There were days I didn't know if I was going to wake up. It was pitch-dark.

My precious mom was diagnosed with stomach cancer, which was basically a death sentence for her. My mom is my hero. She has been both my mom and my dad. Now the doctors were saying they would check her one more time, because if the cancer crept up, she wasn't going to make it.

At the same time, my daughter Amanda was going through challenges with depression and oppression as part of the enemy's attack. She called me when she was at her breaking point, telling me that her life didn't mean anything and she was better off dead. I was on the phone with her praying these devils off because I know my daughter has a powerful calling on her life.

Not only that, but the devil attacked my eyesight again. I have one good eye, the right eye. My left eye has a scar in the back that I got from a snowball fight at the age of sixteen. I can only count fingers through that eye. But now my good eye—the one that allows me to see, travel, preach, get on planes, and go to conferences and events—came under attack.

I lost my vision for six months. I could barely see anything. I remember going to airports and using my iPhone to take pictures, then stretching them to the max so I could see the gate I was leaving from, or asking people for help because I couldn't read the airport signs. I went to doctors, and they told me, "You need major eye surgery, but we can't do anything for you right now."

I dragged on. I held on to the cross, I held on to my faith, and I held on to the good memories—the spiritual ones; memories of all the good things God has done for me. I continued to minister. There were times when I preached what I could see on my iPad and the rest came straight from the heart. I stood through altar calls, bringing people to salvation and casting out devils.

The devil was so angry that my marriage was tested and came under siege as well, to the point that my wife and I lived in two different locations. I couldn't breathe spiritually. I couldn't see in the natural. The devil was coming at me four different ways at once with the fiercest attacks over my life I've ever experienced.

The devil was having the laugh of the day. I'm not ashamed to say I was under attack. There are ministers out there who wear capes and boots, but I don't—I'm dressed up in the Holy Spirit.

On September 25, 2023, I had cataract replacement surgery. I left the hospital two days later, on my way to preach again. I was more determined than the enemy of my soul, the devil. On October 25, 2023, I went for my second surgery, a partial corneal transplant. A week or so later I was on my way to preach. I wanted to finish the year and make Jesus Christ proud. I held on to the words of the Lord in my heart. Even though I was being crushed on every side, I knew He wouldn't give me any more than I could handle.

I couldn't drive for over six months. I was staying in New York and was able to make my way to the stores and delis to buy my meals. My precious sister Cheri, administrator for John Ramirez Ministries, and her daughter would order food for me through a delivery service when I was in California so I could have my next meal.

Today my eyesight is healing; my daughter is in a good place spiritually, and she is seeing the hand of the Lord Jesus Christ move in her life; the Lord removed the hindrance of the devil out of my marriage; and my mom is cancer-free—all praise reports. Only God could make this happen. I praise Him, I worship Him, and I signed up to do life in Jesus without parole. I'm on death row. It's not where you start that's important; it's where you finish.

Praise be to God, the One who called me and ordained me before the foundations of the earth to run this spiritual race, to fight the good fight of faith. Whenever the devil attacks, I am ready to hit the rewind button and remember the goodness of God.

SPIRITUAL DEMENTIA

I want to take you to the Word of God and show you that you're not alone. I have gone through spiritual dementia myself, and I want to testify and help my precious brothers and sisters get this demented devil out of your purpose and your destiny once and for all.

We hear people say these kinds of things all the time:

- "The devil is doing this."
- "The devil is doing that."
- "The devil is defeating me."
- "There is witchcraft on me."
- "The warlock at work is trying to destroy me."
- "My neighbor is doing witchcraft on me."
- "My neighborhood is saturated with witchcraft shops, strongholds, and bondages."
- "There are generational witchcraft curses in my family."
- "The devil is tormenting me with demonic dreams."
- "I feel like I can't move forward."

- "I don't feel Jesus anymore."
- "I feel the Holy Spirit is not with me anymore."
- "I feel like God is not answering my prayers anymore."
- "Does Jesus Christ truly love me?"

Many times when we face spiritual commotion we say "the devil this" and "the devil that" and forget who is in control. How quickly we allow the devil to erase Jesus Christ's name and the Holy Spirit who dwells in us.

I have a news flash for the church: The bad is going to get crazier. But also, the good is going to get awesome. Jesus Christ is coming back soon, and the Holy Spirit is our engagement ring of promise for that big wedding that will happen in heaven. That's the greatest news ever for those who believe in Him, and I'm going to hang my hat on it.

Psalm 30:5 says, "For His anger is but for a moment, His favor is for a lifetime; weeping may last for the night, but a shout of joy comes in the morning" (NASB). What an awesome scripture that is! It has two parts: "Weeping may last for the night," which means it will last only for a season. Don't make permanent decisions based on temporary situations, because the second part of the scripture comes right after: "joy comes in the morning." God's goodness will always show up. God's goodness will always carry you through. God's goodness crushes the head of the serpent, whether the battle is in the world around you or in your personal life.

Today many of us believers have fallen short. We fail to remember the miracles the Lord did yesterday. We fail to see the miracles He is doing in our lives now. We don't expect Him to do miracles tomorrow. But remembering the miracles of God, recalling all the ways He saved you and all the times He came through for you is the weapon you need for today because no matter what you are facing, you know what He is going to do for you tomorrow.

So the next time you're up against the devil, his demonic kingdom, and his cronies, you should say, "If God did it for me yesterday, He's going to do it for me again." This is how you stand in victory knowing that God "is the same yesterday, today, and forever" (Heb. 13:8, NKJV) and His character changes not (Mal. 3:6). Put that in your pocket—or hold it in a basket like the disciples did when they fed the five thousand and there were twelve baskets of food left over. God gave one basket to each of them not because they were hungry but so they would remember the miracles that He did in their lives and not forget His amazing goodness, majesty, and power.

You need to hold on to a basket yourself so in whatever battle you face today or tomorrow you can say, "God did a miracle for me yesterday, He's going to do a miracle for me today, and my miracle is waiting for me tomorrow as well, devil. I know what's in front of me, but God knows what's ahead of me." You can bank on that.

When the Israelites were entering the Promised Land, they had to cross the Jordan River. God performed a miracle for them, holding back the waters of the river so they could cross on dry ground. (See Joshua 3.) Afterward the Lord instructed them to take twelve stones from the middle of the river, one for each tribe. Joshua set up the stones as a reminder to the people of the miracles of the Lord. They were a visible reminder of the power and goodness of God. These were memorial stones. You have memorial stones in your life too, reminders of all the times that God showed up and showed off on your behalf. Don't ever forget them. The stones that represent all the miracles God has done in your life "are to be a memorial...forever" (Josh. 4:7).

Stop Being Spiritually Double-Minded

There are two words that appear for the very first time in the Bible right next door to each other: *sang* and *complained*. Exodus 15:1 says, "Then Moses and the children of Israel sang this song to the LORD" (NKJV). It was the Israelites' first worship and victory song. After they crossed the Red Sea on dry land, after they saw this gigantic miracle, they sang this song:

> I will sing to the LORD, for He has triumphed gloriously! The horse and its rider He has thrown into the sea! The LORD is my strength and song, and He has become my salvation; He is my God, and I will praise Him; my father's God, and I will exalt Him....Pharaoh's chariots and his army He has cast into the sea; his chosen captains also are drowned in the Red Sea. The depths have covered them; they sank to the bottom like a stone.
> —EXODUS 15:1–2, 4–5, NKJV

But just a few verses later we read, "And the people complained against Moses" (Exod. 15:24, NKJV). How could the Israelites go from such an amazing miracle—God parting the waters of the Red Sea so several million people could cross over—to complaining? How is it that the children of Israel crossed on dry ground and sang the first worship song unto the Lord in Exodus 15:1, and then in Exodus 15:24 the people complained? They went from praising the Lord for His miraculous power to murmuring. Just three days after they worshipped God for their dramatic rescue, they were complaining and having an attitude. Considering the magnitude of the miracle they experienced, I would think it would have been at least a year before they opened their mouths to say anything negative. How could you forget a miracle like that—a Red Sea moment?

We need to remember the things the Lord has done. Every Red Sea moment you have had should be a reminder that God can do all things for those who love Him. Every Red Sea moment ahead of you will lead to Marah, the place where God turned bitter water into sweet water. (See Exodus 15:22–25.)

The enemy tries to change the course of our minds to cause us to doubt and lack faith. Sometimes we see a gigantic miracle and then question God about something small three days later. The Israelites were thirsty, and the waters of Marah were bitter. How could they complain about that? If God could open up the Red Sea, He could take bitter water and turn it sweet. But the children of Israel were double-minded, and they chose to complain instead of remembering.

This is also true of believers today. This is the church. We see miracles, signs, and wonders. We hear testimonies of healing. We hear testimonies of deliverance. We hear testimonies of family members or loved ones getting saved when such a thing seemed impossible. We hear testimonies of God stopping accidents. We hear testimonies about loved ones—like my mom—being healed who were sick and gripped by infirmity. When my mom went through cancer, all I knew to do was to pray and remember all the miracles that God has done for me with my eyesight and all the times He has displayed His love for me. I held on to those miracles while I prayed for my mother, and today she is cancer-free!

We see the miracles. We hear the testimonies. We even experience miracles, signs, and wonders ourselves. And we worship the Lord for His goodness, His salvation, His mercy, and His healing.

But then we forget. We doubt. We walk in unbelief. We come across some mediocre challenge, attack, or battle and lose sight of the miraculous things God has done in our lives. God gave us supernatural victory in our wars, but when we come to the small battlefield of bitter waters we murmur and complain, forgetting the song we were singing three days ago. We allow the devil to fragment our minds, and we become double-minded.

James 1:6–8 says, "But when you ask, you must believe and not doubt, because the one who doubts is like a wave of the sea, blown and tossed by the wind. That person should not expect to receive anything from the Lord. Such a person is double-minded and unstable in all they do." Why do we allow the devil to plague us with doubt? How is it that we go from being singing believers to complaining believers from one day to the next? How can we sing praises in one season of victory and question God in the next? How quickly we forget God's miracles, which testify and bring testimonies into our lives. We need to cut out the voices, the distractions, and the enemy's spiritual contradictions that plague us. We need to cut out and uproot the rhetoric of the enemy.

I've got news for you. Whether it's sickness, addiction, or demons tormenting you, when the miracle shows up, you will live in victory. As long as you're breathing, and as long as you declare that Jesus Christ is your Lord and Savior, God will give you a Red Sea moment miracle. But He will test you afterward with a bitter pond or lake called Marah, a bitter attack or moment. He will test you before He makes it sweet again.

As believers we grieve the Holy Spirit, delay the plans of God, and put our purposes and destinies on ice when we believe whatever demonic lies the devil plants in our heads in those times of testing when we come across the bitter water.

Don't let that devil called spiritual dementia creep in. It's time to celebrate God's miracles. It's time to hit the rewind button and let the devil, the kingdom of darkness, and the witches and warlocks know, "You have nothing on me because the God I serve is a miracle-working God. He did it for me yesterday. He did it for me last week. He did it for me last month. He did it for me last year. He did it for me five years ago. He did it for me ten years ago and twenty years ago, and He's here to do it for me again."

Celebrate God's miracles and celebrate His goodness. Stop getting spiritually stuck. Don't let the devil take advantage of you or gain leverage over you.

REMEMBER YOUR SPIRITUAL RÉSUMÉ

Let me bring you to the New Testament.

> These are all warning markers—DANGER!—in our history books, written down so that we don't repeat their mistakes. Our positions in the story are parallel—they at the beginning, we at the end—and we are just as capable of messing it up as they were. Don't be so naive and self-confident. You're not exempt. You could fall flat on your face as easily as anyone else. Forget about self-confidence; it's useless. Cultivate God-confidence.
> —1 CORINTHIANS 10:11–12, MSG

Miracles are meant to be remembered, never forgotten. They are our God-confidence. They are our weapons for getting through the next spiritual warfare battle we face.

The Holy Spirit is teaching us something today: If God performed a miracle for you before, He can do it again. But the devil lives between your miracles. The devil camps between your miracles. The devil waits between your miracles to set you up, discredit the character of God, bring unbelief, and make you doubt that God can do another miracle in your life today.

The story of Jesus feeding the five thousand is a spiritual point of refence, a reminder that as long as you keep your faith in God and your eyes on Jesus Christ, He will never stop doing miracles. That miracle of feeding five thousand souls should have sealed the deal for the disciples, and I'll share with you the reason why so you don't make the same mistake they did.

In Mark 6:34–44 we read:

> When Jesus landed and saw a large crowd, he had compassion on them, because they were like sheep without a shepherd. So he began teaching them many things.
>
> By this time it was late in the day, so his disciples came to him. "This is a remote place," they said, "and it's already very late. Send the people away so that they can go to the surrounding countryside and villages and buy themselves something to eat."
>
> But he answered, "You give them something to eat."
>
> They said to him, "That would take more than half a year's wages! Are we to go and spend that much on bread and give it to them to eat?"
>
> "How many loaves do you have?" he asked. "Go and see."
>
> When they found out, they said, "Five—and two fish."
>
> Then Jesus directed them to have all the people sit down in groups on the green grass. So they sat down in groups of hundreds and fifties. Taking the five loaves and the two fish and looking up to heaven, he gave thanks and broke the loaves. Then he gave them to his disciples to distribute to the people. He also divided the two fish among them all. They all ate and were satisfied, and the disciples picked up twelve basketfuls of broken pieces of bread and fish. The number of the men who had eaten was five thousand.

What an amazing moment! The disciples saw again with their own eyes that God does miracles, and we see it today with our own eyes. When we have spiritual eyes to see, we see that God has done miracle after miracle in our lives. Remember, those miracles that you see in your life are ammunition for your next battle. Why are you allowing the devil to steal your ammunition? Why are you allowing the enemy to rob you? Why are you allowing the enemy to bring spiritual dementia into your walk with Christ, your life, and your spiritual warfare?

Check this out: Right after the disciples gathered up the baskets of leftovers—twelve baskets, one reminder of a miracle for each of them—"Immediately Jesus made his disciples get into the boat and go on ahead of him to Bethsaida" (Mark 6:45). The disciples were in the middle of the water, straining at the oars against the fierce wind, and they once again ended up afraid. The Bible actually says they were "terrified" (v. 50).

Just like the Israelites, the disciples went straight from a big miracle to a test. They had already seen Jesus calm a terrible storm, and right before getting in the boat they had seen Jesus feed thousands of people with a few loaves of bread and two fish. But they were still afraid when they saw Jesus walking on the water. They forgot the other miracles that He had done. Then when Jesus got into the boat, the storm stopped.

Don't limit God. Don't focus so much on the details of the last miracle that you put God in a box by believing the next miracle will happen the same way. When Jesus came walking on the water, it was a new miracle and a new moment for the disciples to see Him in a different way. But instead of celebrating, the disciples were afraid.

Don't miss it; your next miracle is around the corner. Don't confine the Lord and minimize your miracle.

Fast-forward a little bit to Mark 8:1–4:

> During those days another large crowd gathered. Since they
> had nothing to eat, Jesus called his disciples to him and
> said, "I have compassion for these people; they have already
> been with me three days and have nothing to eat. If I send
> them home hungry, they will collapse on the way, because
> some of them have come a long distance."
>
> His disciples answered, "But where in this remote place
> can anyone get enough bread to feed them?"

The disciples said pretty much the same thing they'd said
back in Mark 6. Jesus said the same thing too, telling the disciples to give the people something to eat. It's crazy. The disciples
had already seen the miracle of Jesus feeding the five thousand;
now they were facing the need for another miracle to feed four
thousand people, one thousand fewer than the miracle they had
already witnessed, but still they doubted.

Jesus' response to the disciples was exactly the same as in Mark
6—He asked them, "How many loaves do you have?" (Mark 8:5).
The story continues much like the account of the feeding of the
five thousand:

> "Seven," they replied.
>
> He told the crowd to sit down on the ground. When
> he had taken the seven loaves and given thanks, he broke
> them and gave them to his disciples to distribute to the
> people, and they did so. They had a few small fish as well;
> he gave thanks for them also and told the disciples to dis-
> tribute them. The people ate and were satisfied. Afterward
> the disciples picked up seven basketfuls of broken pieces
> that were left over. About four thousand were present.
>
> —MARK 8:5–9

How did the disciples miss it? This was like a déjà vu moment for them, and they missed it. Man, I think if Jesus had done this miracle in the projects in the South Bronx—if He had fed five thousand people there and then come back a couple days later to do it again—we would have been excited! We would have been jumping up and down and celebrating in anticipation, remembering what He had already done.

Don't Let the Devil Steal Your Miracles

Don't let the devil steal God's miracles out of your life. It's time for you to wake up spiritually and honor the Lord Jesus Christ, bless Him, and glorify His name.

The Lord gives us 86,400 seconds every day. Each of those seconds is a gift. Have you thanked Him for these gifts? Have you stopped and thanked God for the miracles He has done in your life? Don't forget that remembering the miracles of the Lord is your weapon for the next fight, the next battle when the devil shows up and pushes you to question, Will God do it again? Will He show up? Does He hear my prayers?

Don't miss the fact that God gave each of the disciples a basket of leftovers after He fed the five thousand. There were twelve baskets left—one for each of them—and they still failed to remember the blessings and miracles of the Lord. I think that holds a lesson for us.

Don't forget about your basket; hold on to it. When the devil shows up at your next fight, on your next battlefield, you know what to do. You have the mind of Christ (1 Cor. 2:16). You have memories of the goodness of the Lord, and you have testimonies of His miracles. Put the devil on your channel; don't let him put you on his. When the devil attacks you with his lies, take your basket, hold it in his face, and say, "My basket is full of miracles and testimonies. You don't want none of this. You need to step off and take your deception and your demonic dementia somewhere else because I have the mind of Christ." When the enemy shows up to your next fight, hit him over the head with your basketful of miracles.

Have you heard of Formula 409? It's an all-purpose cleaning spray used around the home. The story goes that it was created by two people who lived in Michigan, and they called it Formula 409 because it took them 409 times to get the formula correct.[1] Don't be a 409 Christian who takes 409 times to get it right. Let's get it right the first time. Let's extend our victories to our next victory. Don't allow the devil to live in the in-between by giving in to murmuring, forgetfulness, complaining, or spiritual dementia.

I'm going to sing a song in every battle. Every chance I get, I'm going to sing Moses' song. This is my jam in my miracle times and in my battles. This is how the song goes:

> I will sing to the LORD, for he is highly exalted. Both horse and driver he has hurled into the sea.
>
> The LORD is my strength and my defense; he has become my salvation. He is my God, and I will praise him, my father's God, and I will exalt him. The LORD is a warrior; the LORD is his name. Pharaoh's chariots and his army he has hurled into the sea. The best of Pharaoh's officers are drowned in the Red Sea. The deep waters have covered them; they sank to the depths like a stone. Your right hand, LORD, was majestic in power. Your right hand, LORD, shattered the enemy.
>
> In the greatness of your majesty you threw down those who opposed you. You unleashed your burning anger; it consumed them like stubble. By the blast of your nostrils the waters piled up. The surging waters stood up like a

wall; the deep waters congealed in the heart of the sea. The enemy boasted, "I will pursue, I will overtake them. I will divide the spoils; I will gorge myself on them. I will draw my sword and my hand will destroy them." But you blew with your breath, and the sea covered them. They sank like lead in the mighty waters. Who among the gods is like you, LORD? Who is like you—majestic in holiness, awesome in glory, working wonders?

You stretch out your right hand, and the earth swallows your enemies. In your unfailing love you will lead the people you have redeemed. In your strength you will guide them to your holy dwelling. The nations will hear and tremble....By the power of your arm they will be as still as a stone—until your people pass by, LORD, until the people you bought pass by. You will bring them in and plant them on the mountain of your inheritance—the place, LORD, you made for your dwelling, the sanctuary, LORD, your hands established.

The LORD reigns for ever and ever.

—EXODUS 15:1–14, 16–18

That is our victory song in the One who lives forever, who sits on the circle of the earth, and who's got your back every time. That's my victory song; let it be yours too.

Chapter 3

THE DEVIL'S MINISTRY: TEMPTATION

I ONCE HEARD AN amazing story from my pastor at Times Square Church. There is so much truth behind this story, and it has spiritual meaning as well. This is how the story went.

There was a ship captain who sailed a route from Colombia to California. One day he was unexpectedly approached by a drug cartel, who asked him if he would take a small shipment of drugs to California. They would pay him $500,000. Immediately he declined and told them no. Sometime later they came back and made him another offer. He said no. They kept amping up the offer every single time until they reached two million dollars. He hesitated and said he would think about it. He contacted the DEA in the United States, and they set up a sting operation. The bad guys were arrested. The interesting part of the story is that when the DEA asked him why he waited so long to contact them, the captain responded, "They were getting close to my price."[1]

TEMPTATION HAS A PRICE

Temptation has a price. Temptation comes at a price. Temptation knows your price. Hear me out, loud and clear. I believe that one of the devil's names is Temptation. That is just my take on it. James 1:13 says, "When tempted, no one should say, 'God is tempting me.' For God cannot be tempted by evil, nor does he tempt anyone." God isn't the one tempting you.

Listen to me carefully. I want to teach you. I want to equip you. I want to keep you armed and dangerous. By the power of the Holy Spirit I am exposing the devil and his fine print. Often we read the bigger letters but bypass the fine print—and that is where the danger is. That is where the devil is lurking over you. We see fine print in TV commercials all the time. The company tells you a whole story about something they are selling, but they make the fine print on the television so small you can't even read it, often hiding important information in the fine print. The devil does the same thing.

But I have good news for you today. I'm taking you to the Holy Spirit school. Temptation has a price tag, and here is how it works:

- Temptation knows your weaknesses.
- Temptation knows where you walk and where you are most defenseless.
- Temptation will keep making relentless offers to your soulish man.

One thing you should know about the soulish man is that he is always shopping—not for things of the kingdom of God but for things of the world. The enemy knows that, so he continually makes offers to your soulish man that are enticing, entertaining, and hard to say no to. So what should you do? The Bible says:

No, I strike a blow to my body and make it my slave so that after I have preached to others, I myself will not be disqualified for the prize.

—1 CORINTHIANS 9:27

In other words, the apostle Paul is saying he puts the soulish man, the flesh, the outer man into submission so he will not be disqualified from running the race that God has paved and mapped out for him. We should take heed of Paul's words.

IT'S TIME TO DISARM THE DEVIL AND HIS KINGDOM

I want to teach you where, how, and when the devil comes for you. Every believer should have scriptures on which they hang their hat, and this is where I hang mine.

Isaiah 54:17 says, "No weapon formed against you shall prosper" (NKJV). The word *formed* in that scripture is a personal thing. It means tailor-made or custom-built. The devil knows and understands how to attack, strategize, and come at you with tailor-made and custom-built weapons. The Holy Spirit has given us insight into the artillery and arsenals of the enemy as we face the host of hell.

The battles we face in every season of our lives are custom-built. The enemy uses demonically engineered weapons made specifically to kill, steal, and destroy in order to sabotage your purpose and your destiny. The weapons are designed to attack the areas where you are the weakest spiritually in your relationship with the Lord.

These weapons are not random. They are not generic. The devil is not stupid; he doesn't just step into the ring with you and fight in the dark. He won't go into the battle and fight with some random stuff or something that appeared out of thin air.

The devil and his demons strategize against you and me in the conference room of hell.

Brothers and sisters, it's time to wake up. The trial you're facing today was demonically engineered, custom-built, and tailor-made to bring you down, whether it's sickness, fear, oppression, depression, suicidal thoughts, unrighteous practices, witchcraft, or anything else. The devil is pushing the rewind button to remind you of the life you lived B.C. (before Christ), using thoughts of lust and perversion to try to bring your mind back to Egypt. He has blueprints that show where you are vulnerable, and he strikes like a viper. But I have good news for you today: "No weapon formed against you shall prosper" (Isa. 54:17, NKJV).

It's time to fight back. I'm exposing the devil's playbook. It's time for us to disarm the devil.

Just like the cartel kept making offers to the ship captain, the devil will keep making offers until he finds something that will attract you. When the captain faced temptation, he called the DEA. When we face spiritual temptation, we call on the Holy Spirit.

Don't Take the Bait

Let's hit the rewind button on the enemy and get some answers. Where did he start his ministry? How did he start his ministry? What did he use to present his ministry? Knowing the answers to those questions helps us because the devil is using the same weapons today that he used in the past. The devil's tactics are effective, and he knows how to use his weapons. Two of these weapons in particular have stolen from, killed, and destroyed many people spiritually: the weapon of temptation and the weapon of influence.

This loser called the devil tempted one-third of the angels in heaven with his secret weapon called influence. No sooner was he kicked out of heaven than the devil reinstated his ministry in the Garden of Eden with temptation because that's all he knows. He knows how to play his ace card very well. He ramps up the offers and keeps them enticing, making them nice and sweet. He dresses up as an angel of light to bring these offers until we buy into them, like he did with Adam and Eve.

What I'm about to share with you is my take and my opinion. It's not in the Bible. These are just my thoughts. This is what I think opened the door of temptation for Adam, even though Eve was the first one to take the bait. Adam heard clearly what God told him; the instructions were clear. Adam knew the voice of God perfectly because he spent more time with God than with Eve. Adam's weakness was loneliness. The Bible says Adam was alone and God gave him a helpmate (Gen. 2:18, 20–24). I believe the devil planted a thought in Adam's mind before Eve took the bait: "If you don't listen to her, if you don't obey her, you will lose her."

So when temptation knocked on his door, Adam gave in. When the devil used Eve to make the offer, Adam could have said, "The Lord said we should not eat from this tree," and shut the door on temptation. He could have refused to take the bait, and it would have helped both of them. But because Adam had at one time been lonely, he didn't want to lose the very thing that made him happy. He submitted to Eve instead of submitting to God. Again, this is my opinion, but I saw this kind of thing being practiced in the witchcraft world for twenty-five years. I've seen that kind of witchcraft put on people. It's a lesson to be learned: Don't take the bait.

I don't care what people say to me, even my own wife, my precious daughter, or my mom; when God speaks to me, I have to stand firm. As much as my family loves me and I love them, if they come to me with something that's totally opposite what I heard from God, I have to draw the line with love in order to keep the devil from coming in to ruin us all.

I say this with a heavy heart: the devil has stolen many ministers and their ministries because the ministers took the bait. Pastors with awesome callings and incredible anointing in their lives have fallen into the trap. They have given up their ministries, their churches, and their duties in the kingdom. But it's time to fight back. There is no reason to surrender, give in, or give up. The devil is weak, limited, and defeated. I'm exposing the devil's playbook and his demonic arsenal. It doesn't matter if his weapons are tailor-made, custom-built, and satanically engineered—"No weapon formed against you shall prosper" (Isa. 54:17, NKJV).

Devil, I'm Your Huckleberry

Spiritual warfare is like the interaction between a cat and a mouse. The cat can have the mouse cornered, and the mouse knows deep down inside he is defeated and going to be lunch any minute, but he still shows off his teeth and his claws, hoping that will chase the cat away. That is the only thing he can do to try to save his life.

It's the same with the devil—and the devil is the mouse. Deep down he knows he is already defeated, but he will show his teeth and his claws through temptation because that's the only way he can grip us and put strongholds and bondages in our lives.

In order for temptation to be temptation, it has to attract you spiritually. It has to be something that you want. Temptation is demonic bait designed to incarcerate you, dominate you, control you, and eventually kill you spiritually.

The devil even tried to tempt Jesus. The three temptations the devil used wouldn't have been temptations if he hadn't been after anything. He was trying to set Jesus up.

> Then Jesus was led by the Spirit into the wilderness to be tempted by the devil. After fasting forty days and forty nights, he was hungry. The tempter came to him and said, "If you are the Son of God, tell these stones to become bread."
>
> Jesus answered, "It is written: 'Man shall not live on bread alone, but on every word that comes from the mouth of God.'"
>
> Then the devil took him to the holy city and had him stand on the highest point of the temple. "If you are the Son of God," he said, "throw yourself down. For it is written: 'He will command his angels concerning you, and they will lift you up in their hands, so that you will not strike your foot against a stone.'"
>
> Jesus answered him, "It is also written: 'Do not put the Lord your God to the test.'"
>
> Again, the devil took him to a very high mountain and showed him all the kingdoms of the world and their splendor. "All this I will give you," he said, "if you will bow down and worship me."
>
> Jesus said to him, "Away from me, Satan! For it is written: 'Worship the Lord your God, and serve him only.'"
>
> Then the devil left him, and angels came and attended him.
>
> —MATTHEW 4:1–11

In this passage of Scripture the devil was trying to push Jesus to make premature decisions. He was trying to distract Jesus and keep Him away from the path of the cross. Hebrews 4:15 says, "For we do not have a high priest who is unable to empathize with our weaknesses, but we have one who has been tempted in every way, just as we are—yet he did not sin." How powerful is that! Jesus was tempted just like we are, but He didn't sin. He used the Word to fight back against the devil.

The devil had a piece of fruit to tempt Eve. He had grapes for Noah because Noah was a drunk. He had thirty pieces of silver for Judas, a traitor. He had a window for David, leading him to lust and murder. He had a lying spirit for Peter, who denied Jesus three times. He had seven hundred wives and three hundred concubines for King Solomon that brought him to destruction. The devil knows which of your weaknesses to exploit to draw you into temptation. Whatever it is, you need to kill it spiritually before it kills you. Use these powerful prayers:

- Satan, listen to me. I put you on notice by the power of the blood of Jesus. I am a child of God, and I sit in heavenly places. (See Ephesians 2:6.)

- Through the power of the name of Jesus I quench every satanic darkness and fiery dart against me today, in my season, and in the season to come. (See Ephesians 6:16.)

- Devil, I am more than a conqueror because greater is He that lives in me than he that lives in the world. (See Romans 8:37 and 1 John 4:4.)

- I confess that I am a child of God, and I stand in the Word of God. I stand on the truth of God. Devil, I stand in triumph to win over every temptation that you use to gain leverage over me, whether in my blind spot, in front of me, or behind me. I crush the head of the serpent today in Jesus' mighty name. Amen. (See Genesis 3:15.)

- Devil, I remind you today and put you on notice:
  I'm not the old person anymore. I am a new crea-
  ture. I can do all things through Christ who gives
  me the strength to crush your head all day and
  every day, in this season and the one to come. In
  Jesus' awesome name, amen. (See 2 Corinthians 5:17
  and Philippians 4:13.)

- I am anointed because of the Holy Spirit dwelling
  inside of me; therefore, every yoke, every bondage,
  and every stronghold will fall off me today, shrivel
  up and die, and be destroyed because of the
  anointing in Jesus' incredible, awesome name.
  Amen.

- I baptize myself with the blessings of the Lord. I
  declare I am blessed and not cursed. I will live
  and not die. In Jesus' awesome, all-powerful name,
  amen.

The Bible says in 2 Corinthians 2:11, "...lest Satan should take advantage of us. For we are not ignorant of his devices" (MEV). God doesn't want you to be ignorant of the devil's devices. The devil goes after the areas where you are vulnerable, receptive, and defenseless. He goes after the areas in which you have weaknesses. Cover those areas. Protect those areas. Submit those areas to the Holy Spirit. If you do that, when the tailor-made, custom-built weapons show up, they won't find a target in you. They won't move you. They won't shake you. They won't dominate you. They won't incarcerate you.

Spiritual Nuggets and Spiritual Wisdom

What is temptation? Temptation is a fork in the road, a place where you have to choose which way to go. Temptation feeds on your curiosity, so be aware.

The word *temptation* comes from a word that simply means a test.[2] Temptation is a test to prove to God that you love Him above everything else.

Jesus said, "It is written," three times while He was being tempted by Satan. Every one of His "It is written" statements came from the same book of the Bible: Deuteronomy. Deuteronomy may not be a book that excites us, but Jesus beat the devil with it three times. Jesus didn't face a little demon in the wilderness. He didn't face Julio or Fred or Crazy Wanda or Crazy Daisy. He didn't face a little warlock or a little witch. He faced the devil himself and took him out with the Book of Deuteronomy. How awesome is that!

This shows us we can beat down the devil with all sixty-six books of the Bible. I think this is a moment for a *hallelujah*! This is a shouting moment. You should be jumping out of your seat, running around your apartment or your house with this revelation!

I have awesome news for you. The Bible says the same presence and power of the Holy Spirit that enabled Jesus to resist temptation lives in every Christian. We were made by the hands of Jesus Christ to be overcomers. No weapon formed against us will prosper.

The Bible says in 1 Corinthians 10:13, "No temptation has overtaken you except such as is common to man; but God is faithful, who will not allow you to be tempted beyond what you are able, but with the temptation will also make the way of escape, that you may be able to bear it" (NKJV). Christ was tempted, so we will be tempted. Christ overcame, so we can overcome: "You are of God, little children, and have overcome them, because He who is in you is greater than he who is in the world" (1 John 4:4, MEV). With every temptation, He will provide the escape route. Always look for that spiritual door.

Read this amazing quote from R. A. Torrey:

> Contemplate the temptations you are likely to face during the day; ask God to reveal these to you and grant you the strength for victory over these temptations before they come. Many people fail because they wait until the hour of battle to prepare. However, those who succeed do so because they have won their victory in prayer before the battle even begins....Anticipate your battles, fight them in prayer before temptation arrives, and you will always achieve victory.[3]

You can take that to the bank.

Here is something else you need to know: a Wordless Christian is a powerless Christian. Think about it. If Jesus needed the Word of God to defeat the devil, what makes you think you can do it without the Word?

Another trick of the enemy, another one of his schemes, is how he manipulates and controls your thoughts. I have a spiritual rule: if any thought enters my mind that contradicts or challenges the Word of God, that brings chaos or brings no peace, I have thirty seconds to destroy it, take it out of my mind, dismiss it, and uproot it completely and fully—because it has temptation written all over it. Also, the Word tells us to bring "every thought into captivity to the obedience of Christ" (2 Cor. 10:5, NKJV).

I've known precious believers who served the Lord for years with all their hearts and were on fire, devoted, and dedicated, but then they fell away. What happened? I saw their walk, I saw their fruit, and I saw the power of God in their lives, but now they're back in the world.

I will tell you what happened: The devil planted thoughts in their minds that were tailor-made to steal, kill, and destroy, and these satanically engineered thoughts were never uprooted but instead lay dormant. Then one day those thoughts sprang up and took over. There have been many well-known ministers, apostles, pastors, and leaders of the faith who believed in Jesus Christ 100 percent, but they didn't destroy those thoughts from the devil, so they drifted into a demonic atmosphere. Some even ended up preaching a gospel that was not the gospel of Christ at all.

The devil has used temptation to wrap himself around many people's thoughts, tempting them to be something God never called them to be, to run a race they weren't supposed to run, or to become influential or popular. When we wrap ourselves in the garments of those temptations, we drift away from the very spot where God placed us. This is what the apostle Paul warned us about in the Book of Galatians:

> I marvel that you are turning away so soon from Him who called you in the grace of Christ, to a different gospel, which is not another; but there are some who trouble you and want to pervert the gospel of Christ. But even if we, or an angel from heaven, preach any other gospel to you than what we have preached to you, let him be accursed. As we have said before, so now I say again, if anyone preaches any other gospel to you than what you have received, let him be accursed.
>
> —GALATIANS 1:6–9, NKJV

We must take control of our thoughts. Charles Spurgeon said, "If you will tell me when God permits a Christian to lay aside his armour, I will tell you when Satan has left off temptation.

Like the old knights in war time, we must sleep with helmet and breastplate buckled on, for the arch-deceiver will seize our first unguarded hour to make us his prey."[4]

Know this, my brothers and sisters: if God were not my friend, Satan would not be my enemy. The day you made God your friend, the devil put a bull's-eye on your back. First Peter 5:8 says, "Be alert and of sober mind. Your enemy the devil prowls around like a roaring lion looking for someone to devour." I refuse to be the devil's lunch.

I learned something by watching the Discovery channel. In order for a lion's hunt to be successful, the lion must stalk its prey before it attacks. That is the devil's game. He stalks you to learn your weaknesses before he attacks. I also learned that when people are out on a safari, they keep the fires going all night long because the fire keeps the lions out. If the fire goes out, the lions come in.

The devil can only come to devour you when you let your fire go out. So how do you keep the fire burning?

- Fear God.

- Reverence Him.

- Be mindful of Him. How can God give us 86,400 seconds a day and we use none of those 86,400 seconds to talk to Him, acknowledge Him, worship Him, or be thankful and show gratitude for all the good things He has done for us?

- Read and meditate on the Word of God. Get it in your mind, and let the Holy Spirit write it on your heart.

That's how you keep your spiritual fire going. Don't be spiritually careless. Becoming lukewarm is dangerous. Revelation 3:16 (NKJV) says, "So then, because you are lukewarm, and neither cold nor hot, I will vomit you out of My mouth."

You might ask, "Hey, John, how do I know if I'm lukewarm?" That is a good question. When you are lukewarm, you still believe in Jesus, but you're not as excited about Him as you once were. It's time to get desperate for Jesus and be more determined than the devil. Get your fight back on.

We are in a battle. I know this well—when Christ is nearest, the devil is the busiest. The whisper of temptation is knocking at the door. Matthew 26:41 says, "Watch and pray so that you will not fall into temptation. The spirit is willing, but the flesh is weak." James 4:7 says, "Submit yourselves, then, to God. Resist the devil, and he will flee from you." Submitting to God is key. When you submit to Him, you recognize God's authority over your life.

You will always be tempted. You can't be delivered from being tempted, but you can be victorious and not give in. Let's not commit spiritual suicide. Let's make Jesus Christ proud that He picked us for the battle. Isaiah 54:17 says, "No weapon formed against you shall prosper" (NKJV). We are victorious (1 Cor. 15:57). "We are more than conquerors" (Rom. 8:37). We are the head and not the tail (Deut. 28:13). We are the righteousness of Christ Jesus (2 Cor. 5:21). We are armed and dangerous, and we're here to let the devil know, "Stay where you're at; we're coming for you."

Chapter 4

EPHESIANS 6: THE ULTIMATE FIGHT

MONG THE FIRST words recorded in the Word of the Lord in Genesis is a question of doubt that spilled out of the devil's mouth. Genesis 3:1 says, "Now the serpent was more crafty than any of the wild animals the LORD God had made. He said to the woman, 'Did God really say, "You must not eat from any tree in the garden"?'"

We are challenged in every aspect of our walk with the Lord Jesus Christ. That same question pops up in our minds today. The devil's playbook is filled with questions designed to cause us to doubt:

- Did God really say that?

- Is God really speaking to me?

- Is all of God's Word really true?

- Does God's Word really mean what it says?

- Did I hear from God?

- Is this my mind or my conscience instead of God?

- Will God answer my prayers?

- Will God set me free?

41

- Will God heal me from my sickness?

I would like to share a spiritual nugget with you that has been impactful in my life. The devil loves to bring difficulty in our Christian walks and our seasons of life to confuse us and complicate things spiritually so we will make permanent decisions based on temporary situations. They are called spiritual setbacks. Listen to me carefully with your spiritual ears: Difficulty is not directional. You don't have to relocate just because you're in a battle. Many times when we have difficulties in our lives, it means God is using our situation to deepen us in the season we're in.

Your first prayer when facing difficulties should be for God's timing. Your second prayer should be for purpose. In other words, I'm praying for the timing of the Lord upon my life, my season, and my difficulty. I'm praying to know when to move and how to move in the Spirit, to be led by the Holy Spirit into my next purpose and my next season so I can be prepared and equipped for the next battle and the next blessing. That's how I pray. I pray this will be a blessing to you as well, in Jesus' mighty name.

We will always have to deal with doubt, that questioning of God that was ingrafted from the beginning of time. The devil knows how to play his demonic deck of cards against the believer today. I hear it all the time during my altar calls. I hear it from precious brothers and sisters who are really in love with the Lord Jesus Christ.

Doubt plagues us day in and day out, especially when we're moving from one season to another. The enemy poured doubt into Eve's heart, and he uses the same tactics with us. We have victories in the battle and the blessings of our Lord Jesus Christ right in front of us, but we allow the enemy to get comfortable in the best chair in the living room of our mind. We allow the devil to sit there and spit out, "Did God really say...? Do you really think He is going to heal you? Is He really going to set you free? Look at yourself. You've been in this situation for years. You prayed and you fasted, but you are still stuck." He says these things so doubt will become a stronghold in your mind and fear will keep you in bondage.

As long as you continue to let the enemy sit in the living room of your mind, you give him the remote control of your mental television. You will face attacks on your family, your children, your loved ones, and even your marriage. There are doubts. There are fears. All that is the result of the devil simply saying what he has repeated for thousands of years: "Did God really say...?" It is the giant question mark of the demonic world, making you think there is a *maybe*, a *what if*, or an *if so* behind what God spoke to you.

When God speaks, it's *yes*, *no*, or *hold on*. There is no question mark with our Lord Jesus Christ. So pay attention to where the devil is sitting so you can see where he is trying to ambush you spiritually. He sits between your blessing and your battlefield—we are blessed and in a battle at the same time.

BE A SPIRITUAL MMA FIGHTER

Where are the Nehemiahs in the body of Christ today? Where are the believers who fight with one hand and build the kingdom with the other? I'm blessed that God picked me to build the kingdom on the earth and help rebuild the walls of the church that the devil has torn down, leaving us exposed, wretched, in despair, and spiritually depleted. We need to fight the good fight, punching the devil in the face with one hand and building the biblical principles of the kingdom, the sound doctrines in the Word of God, with the other.

We need to have a relationship with the Lord, not religion. God is always up to something, and the devil is always trying to stop it. The only reason we face intense battles is because God wants to bring about incredible victories in our lives.

Remember this key from the Book of Ephesians: "For our struggle is not against flesh and blood, but against the rulers, against the authorities, against the powers of this dark world and against the spiritual forces of evil in the heavenly realms" (6:12). Many people just focus on the spiritual armor of God in Ephesians 6, but all six chapters of the book are important. Don't discard the rest of the book; that is a sign to the devil that you are immature and lack understanding.

All six chapters of the Book of Ephesians say something about spiritual identity, spiritual blessings, spiritual wisdom, spiritual knowledge, and spiritual richness in Christ. I'm not talking about boats, houses, cars, helicopters, and jets; the world has those. Our focus should be on those things that the world doesn't have, the things we need from a heavenly perspective. We need to keep our eyes on the prize, on the finished work of the cross. We need victory in the lives of our families and loved ones, in our ministries, our purposes, and our destinies. Those are the things that matter.

Many times on the roller coaster of your spiritual life you may find yourself with no answers and no one to talk to. But I want to let you know you're still sitting in heavenly places. "He raised us up and seated us together in the heavenly places in Christ Jesus" (Eph. 2:6, MEV). That's where the fight is. That is where we beat the devil. That is where we destroy the works of darkness. That's where we rattle the devil's cage.

We are seated in heavenly places, which explains how battles and blessings happen all at one time. One day you find yourself on the mountaintop having a Peppermint Pattie with Jesus; the next moment you find yourself in the valley in a battle for your spiritual life. We want Jesus to bless us, but we don't want battles. Every blessing comes with a battle.

A principle of battle is to stop asking God your Lord and Savior to remove things from your life, your season, your trial, or your testing. The devil laughs at believers when we do this. God says, "Shut the devil's mouth. Punch him in the teeth. Kick him in the stomach." Every blessing sits in heavenly places, and we have to go get them. We need to be MMA fighters spiritually and put the devil under submission once and for all.

THE DEVIL'S MOUTHPIECE

When you hear something thousands of times, it's easy to believe it. But some things we hear over and over again come from the lips of the devil. They are words of deception, saying things in a different way than God says them. I heard a certain statement many times as a young believer, and even today I hear people repeat it without having a clue that they are speaking for the devil's kingdom and not the kingdom of Jesus Christ: "You are so heavenly minded that you are of no earthly good."

Let me tell you, I don't believe that at all. Those are the words of the devil meant to disarm and deceive you. Listen instead to the Word of God:

> Since, then, you have been raised with Christ, set your hearts on things above, where Christ is, seated at the right hand of God. Set your minds on things above, not on earthly things. For you died, and your life is now hidden with Christ in God.
>
> —COLOSSIANS 3:1–3

The only way we can be of earthly good is to be heavenly minded. Don't let the devil twist that on you. When you believe or repeat that you can be so heavenly minded that you are of no earthly good, and you decide to walk it out, you're fighting the devil in the natural. You're fighting the devil on his territory, on his turf, on his playground, and in his schoolyard. The Lord tells us, "Set your hearts on things above, where Christ is, seated at the right hand of God" (v. 1). This is how we live. This is how we fight. This is how we get our victories. This is how we own our blessings.

Read the same Scripture passage from *The Message*:

> So if you're serious about living this new resurrection life with Christ, *act* like it. Pursue the things over which Christ presides. Don't shuffle along, eyes to the ground, absorbed with the things right in front of you. Look up, and be alert to what is going on around Christ—that's where the action is. See things from *his* perspective.
>
> Your old life is dead. Your new life, which is your *real* life—even though invisible to spectators—is with Christ in God. *He* is your life. When Christ (your real life, remember) shows up again on this earth, you'll show up, too—the real you, the glorious you. Meanwhile, be content with obscurity, like Christ.

Let's change the channel of spiritual warfare starting now. Set your spiritual eyes on things above, in heavenly places. Draw the devil into your territory, don't let him draw you into his—the things that we see, the things that are natural, the things that bring fear and doubt. "Did God really say...?" The devil is a liar. We fight from heavenly places.

Second Corinthians 4:18 says, "So we fix our eyes not on what is seen, but on what is unseen, since what is seen is temporary, but what is unseen is eternal." The devil doesn't want you to have spiritual eyes and discernment. It's time to use the weapons of our warfare in the heavenly places, where Christ sits at the right hand of the Father.

As soon as you say yes to Jesus, the battle is on. Many of us don't want to say yes. We want the blessings of the heavenly places, but we don't want to say yes because we're afraid and intimidated. But I'm going into the battle to represent Jesus Christ at any cost, and He's on the battlefield with me because I invite Him to every battle, every moment of my life.

My blessings are not at the mall. They are not at the car dealership or an open house. These things are good, but they are not heavenly places. That is why we need to pray, "Lord, open my spiritual eyes." James 4:2 says, "You do not have because you do not ask God." In other words, we ask not, so we get not.

Second Kings 6:15–18 says:

> When the servant of the man of God got up and went out early the next morning, an army with horses and chariots had surrounded the city. "Oh no, my lord! What shall we do?" the servant asked.
>
> "Don't be afraid," the prophet answered. "Those who are with us are more than those who are with them."
>
> And Elisha prayed, "Open his eyes, LORD, so that he may see." Then the LORD opened the servant's eyes, and he looked and saw the hills full of horses and chariots of fire all around Elisha.
>
> As the enemy came down toward him, Elisha prayed to the LORD, "Strike this army with blindness." So he struck them with blindness, as Elisha had asked.

My prayer for you, my brothers and sisters whom I love with all my heart, is that your eyes will be opened. Stop listening to lying pastors and leaders. If all they are interested in is getting you to sow a thousand-dollar seed so you can get a husband or a wife, I have news for you: all you're going to get for that thousand dollars is a Crazy Willie or a Dizzy Daisy. Pastors and leaders like that don't care about your spiritual well-being. They don't care if you make it. They don't care if you finish. They don't care if you move from glory to glory. You need spiritual eyes and discernment.

The Bible doesn't lie. The Word of God stands forever (Isa. 40:8). We fight from heavenly places. We fight battles from a position of authority, from a position of victory, as more than conquerors: "No, in all these things we are more than conquerors through him who loved us" (Rom. 8:37). You need to understand these things in the spirit, and I pray that the Holy Spirit will give you revelation and clarity. We don't look to men. We look to God.

> I lift up my eyes to the mountains—where does my help come from? My help comes from the LORD, the Maker of heaven and earth. He will not let your foot slip—he who watches over you will not slumber; indeed, he who watches over Israel will neither slumber nor sleep. The LORD watches over you—the LORD is your shade at your right hand; the sun will not harm you by day, nor the moon by night. The LORD will keep you from all harm—he will watch over your life; the LORD will watch over your coming and going both now and forevermore.
>
> —PSALM 121

Stop believing the devil when he says, "Did God really say...?" Ephesians 1:3 says, "Praise be to the God and Father of our Lord Jesus Christ, who has blessed us in the heavenly realms with every spiritual blessing in Christ." That's where we start. That's the position we fight from. Heavenly places are where the fight is and where the blessings are. The devil wants you to believe you are fighting from a place that he can control and dominate, but that is just deception.

Stop trying to fight the devil down here on earth with your natural eyes, with your soulish man. You're losing the fight. You're losing the battle. That's why you have spiritual turbulence in your life. You need to go higher and deeper and fight from heavenly places.

STOP RELOCATING

Did you know that blessings and the demonic forces from hell live on the same street? The street is called heavenly places. All the devils you are fighting hang out in heavenly places—the devils you are fighting at work, in your life, in your marriage, to be healed, for your family to be saved, for your purpose and destiny to be revealed to you, and to break out of spiritual poverty or financial poverty, as well as bloodline devils, generational curse devils, and even the ones inside the counterfeit, copycat, bootleg Christians and leaders.

The apostle Paul warned us of these things: "I know that after I leave, savage wolves will come in among you and will not spare the flock" (Acts 20:29). Please understand that I'm not talking about flesh and blood. Remember, Ephesians 6:12 says, "For our struggle is not against flesh and blood, but against the rulers, against the authorities, against the powers of this dark world and against the spiritual forces of evil in the heavenly realms." By the inspiration of the Holy Spirit, I'm giving you a window to see into the heavenly places; to see spiritual activity, the spiritual battleground, and spiritual atmospheres. These are spiritual nuggets that we need in order to understand Ephesians 6:12 and the devils that live in the heavenly realms.

Heavenly places, or *heavenly realms*, refers to an unseen world where spiritual conflict takes place, where we are seated with Christ. This place is more real than the air you breathe. It is so important that it is mentioned five times in just the Book of Ephesians. It is important to our Lord Jesus Christ for us to know and understand and walk in victory. That is why we need the spiritual insight about what happens in heavenly places.

Let's look at some examples in the Scriptures. Daniel 10:2–3 says, "At that time I, Daniel, mourned for three weeks. I ate no choice food; no meat or wine touched my lips; and I used no lotions at all until the three weeks were over." Daniel was praying and believing God, but his answer was delayed. An angel finally appeared and told him:

> Daniel, you who are highly esteemed, consider carefully the words I am about to speak to you, and stand up, for I have now been sent to you....Do not be afraid, Daniel. Since the first day that you set your mind to gain understanding and to humble yourself before your God, your words were heard, and I have come in response to them. But the prince of the Persian kingdom resisted me twenty-one days. Then Michael, one of the chief princes, came to help me, because I was detained there with the king of Persia.
> —DANIEL 10:11–13

It's crazy that Daniel's prayers were answered the first day he prayed, but his blessing wasn't delivered until twenty-one days later. How many blessings do we have in the heavenly places that are being interrupted or intercepted by demonic forces because we don't know how to fight in the heavenly places? We shrink back and listen to the lies of the enemy that God is not hearing or answering or receiving our prayers. When the devil comes at you with those lies, tell him to his face, "Heavenly places—I'll meet you there."

Let's look at another example:

> Then he showed me Joshua the high priest standing before the angel of the LORD, and Satan standing at his right side to accuse him. The LORD said to Satan, "The LORD rebuke you, Satan! The LORD, who has chosen Jerusalem, rebuke you! Is not this man a burning stick snatched from the fire?"
>
> Now Joshua was dressed in filthy clothes as he stood before the angel. The angel said to those who were standing before him, "Take off his filthy clothes."
>
> Then he said to Joshua, "See, I have taken away your sin, and I will put fine garments on you."
>
> Then I said, "Put a clean turban on his head." So they put a clean turban on his head and clothed him, while the angel of the LORD stood by.
>
> —ZECHARIAH 3:1–5

That's us in heavenly places. God has purified us, sanctified us, and dressed us up eternally for the fight, for the battle, and for His glory. But when the battles come, the devil still lies about you. The Bible calls him "the father of lies" (John 8:44) and "the accuser of our brethren" (Rev. 12:10, NKJV). Because you tapped into heavenly places, he's trying to trick you, deceive you, and remove you from that position by lying about you and about the character of our Lord Jesus Christ. He is trying to diminish and tarnish God's character so he can move you to the earthly realm—that's how he can gain leverage and conquer you. Don't let the devil win. It's time to get rid of the guilt and shame. It's time to fight.

Let's look at one more passage of Scripture about heavenly places:

> One day the angels came to present themselves before the LORD, and Satan also came with them. The LORD said to Satan, "Where have you come from?"
>
> Satan answered the LORD, "From roaming throughout the earth, going back and forth on it."
>
> Then the LORD said to Satan, "Have you considered my servant Job? There is no one on earth like him; he is blameless and upright, a man who fears God and shuns evil."
>
> "Does Job fear God for nothing?" Satan replied. "Have you not put a hedge around him and his household and everything he has? You have blessed the work of his hands, so that his flocks and herds are spread throughout the land. But now stretch out your hand and strike everything he has, and he will surely curse you to your face."
>
> The LORD said to Satan, "Very well, then, everything he has is in your power, but on the man himself do not lay a finger."
>
> —JOB 1:6–12

This conversation took place in the heavenly places. If you are a follower of Jesus Christ, you can take Job's name out of this passage and replace it with yours. Let's get one thing straight: Satan is not the CEO. He can't make decisions over your life and mine on his own. God has put limits on him, even in the battlefield, even when you are under attack. God is King over your life yesterday, today, and forever. God is always in control.

Don't listen to the devil when he says, "Did God really say…?" Throw that in the dumpster. Keep the truth in your heart that you are blessed and in the battle at the same time. Don't try to relocate just because you are in a battle. Every blessing is surrounded by demonic forces. Be heavenly minded so you can be of earthly good.

If you understand something in your spirit, you will catch it in your spirit. Be like the people of Israel in the Book of Nehemiah "who were building the wall. Those who carried materials did their work with one hand and held a weapon in the other" (4:17). That should be your story.

Decree that we live in heavenly places. Decree:

> We believe in one God, the Father, the Almighty, maker of heaven and earth, of all that is, seen and unseen.
>
> We believe in one Lord, Jesus Christ, the only Son of God, eternally begotten of the Father, God from God, Light from Light, true God from true God, begotten, not made, of one Being with the Father. Through him all things were made. For us and for our salvation he came down from heaven: by the power of the Holy Spirit he became incarnate from the Virgin Mary, and was made man. For our sake he was crucified under Pontius Pilate; he suffered death and was buried. On the third day he rose again in accordance with the Scriptures; he ascended into heaven and is seated at the right hand of the Father. He will come again in glory to judge the living and the dead, and his kingdom will have no end.
>
> We believe in the Holy Spirit, the Lord, the giver of life, who proceeds from the Father and the Son. With the Father and the Son he is worshiped and glorified. He has spoken through the Prophets. We believe in one holy catholic and apostolic Church. We acknowledge one baptism for the forgiveness of sins. We look for the resurrection of the dead, and the life of the world to come. Amen.[1]

That's how we roll. That's how we live. That's who we are. The recipe is not only to live in heavenly places but also to destroy and conquer every demonic kingdom, system, and attack that comes your way. Never fight the devil in his natural territory.

If you are thinking, seeing, and speaking from your soulish man or your outer man, you will never beat the devil. We don't fight by sight; we fight by faith (2 Cor. 5:7). We don't fight with a carnal mindset but with the mind of Christ (1 Cor. 2:16). If you don't fight by faith and with the mind of Christ, the devil will take over and own every season of your spiritual life. Your eyes, your thoughts, your heart, and your emotions are doors of your outer man in the natural. If the devil can control your mind, he can own it through worries, fears, sickness, doubt, and unbelief. It will be the spiritual poison he uses to finish you off.

The devil can't spiritually breathe in the heavenly places, so consider yourself like an eagle. When an eagle catches a snake, he takes it to his battlefield, to the sky, high above the environment the snake is used to, high above where the snake is powerful and deadly. Then the eagle releases the snake from up in the sky. The snake has no power, no stamina, and no balance; he is useless. The same is true of the devil when we fight him in heavenly places.

Your fight is in heavenly places. The reason you're having spiritual turbulence is because you're trying to fight the devil in his atmosphere and his comfort zone. Change the battleground; if you change the battleground, you change the atmosphere. Invite Christ into the equation. Take your fight into the heavenly places.

Chapter 5

I HAVE NOTHING LEFT TO GIVE, LORD

S OMETIMES THE DEVIL isolates you by separating you from your church and your fellowship with precious brothers and sisters. You end up in a season when you feel like you have nothing left to give to the Lord because you're spiritually empty, depleted, exhausted, burnt out, and drained.

In 2023 I experienced that kind of season in my life. After twenty-four years of walking with the Lord, I came to the point where I said, "I have nothing left to give, Lord. Help me." All I saw was darkness and the hosts of hell coming from every direction. It was one piece of bad news after the other: the situation with my eyes, my mom's health, my daughter's depression, and my marriage being under siege.

You may be saying, "I've got nothing left to give, Lord." If so, you are not alone. You are not the only one who has ever gone through a season like that. And I have good news for you: you will be an overcomer before this chapter is over.

Psalm 42 says:

As the deer pants for streams of water, so my soul pants for you, my God. My soul thirsts for God, for the living God. When can I go and meet with God? My tears have been my food day and night, while people say to me all day long, "Where is your God?" These things I remember as I pour out my soul: how I used to go to the house of God under the protection of the Mighty One with shouts of joy and praise among the festive throng.

Why, my soul, are you downcast? Why so disturbed within me? Put your hope in God, for I will yet praise him, my Savior and my God. My soul is downcast within me; therefore I will remember you from the land of the Jordan, the heights of Hermon—from Mount Mizar. Deep calls to deep in the roar of your waterfalls; all your waves and breakers have swept over me. By day the LORD directs his love, at night his song is with me—a prayer to the God of my life.

I say to God my Rock, "Why have you forgotten me? Why must I go about mourning, oppressed by the enemy?" My bones suffer mortal agony as my foes taunt me, saying to me all day long, "Where is your God?"

Why, my soul, are you downcast? Why so disturbed within me? Put your hope in God, for I will yet praise him, my Savior and my God.

This was the cry of the psalmist. He was in the same place in which you may find yourself today, and the place in which I found myself in 2023. But the psalmist knew what to do. He knew where to put his hope and his faith.

My precious brothers and sisters, you may want to give up right now. You may want to throw in the towel. You may be exhausted, drained, and fatigued. You may feel like you have nothing left to give to the Lord. But there is hope.

Be More Determined Than the Devil—Keep Knocking

In the Book of Luke, right after Jesus taught the Lord's Prayer, He told an amazing story:

> Suppose one of you has a friend, and goes to him at midnight and says to him, "Friend, lend me three loaves, because a friend of mine has come to me from a journey and I have nothing to serve him"; and from inside he answers and says, "Do not bother me; the door has already been shut and my children and I are in bed; I cannot get up and give you anything." I tell you, even if he will not get up and give him anything just because he is his friend, yet because of his shamelessness he will get up and give him as much as he needs. So I say to you, ask, and it will be given to you; seek, and you will find; knock, and it will be opened to you. For everyone who asks receives, and the one who seeks finds, and to the one who knocks, it will be opened.
>
> —LUKE 11:5–10, NASB

There is a spiritual warfare lesson in this precious parable. There is so much insight, so much revelation. There is hope, there is courage, and there is victory in this passage of Scripture. Whatever you're facing spiritually today, it fits in the big picture of this parable.

A man asks a friend for food, but the friend doesn't have anything to give. The friend goes to the house of another friend, asking him to open up his pantry so he can bless his other friend. You have one guy who is hungry, one who is breadless, and one who has the bread. One needs something, one has nothing, and one has everything.

When the one who needs bread to give his friend knocks on the door, he pleads with his friend, "I have nothing." He's overwhelmed. He asks for three loaves of bread—he asks big and isn't shy, even though it is an inconvenient time. This is a picture of us when we are overwhelmed spiritually, when we feel like we have nothing left to give. But there is a friend with all the bread you need. There is One who can fill every need you have. So you can ask big, knowing there is no such thing as an inconvenient time with Jesus.

I love what the late Charles Stanley said: "The shortest distance between our problems and their solutions is the distance between our knees and the floor."[1] Don't let the devil keep you distracted. The enemy knows that when you fall on your knees, heaven moves on your behalf.

Don't Let the Devil Steal Your Victory

Read this story about the apostle Paul and Silas in Acts 16:22–28 (NKJV):

> Then the multitude rose up together against [Paul and Silas]; and the magistrates tore off their clothes and commanded them to be beaten with rods. And when they had laid many stripes on them, they threw them into prison, commanding the jailer to keep them securely. Having received such a charge, he put them into the inner prison and fastened their feet in the stocks.
>
> But at midnight Paul and Silas were praying and singing hymns to God, and the prisoners were listening to them. Suddenly there was a great earthquake, so that the foundations of the prison were shaken; and immediately all the doors were opened and everyone's chains were loosed. And the keeper of the prison, awaking from sleep and seeing the prison doors open, supposing the prisoners had fled, drew his sword and was about to kill himself. But Paul called

with a loud voice, saying, "Do yourself no harm, for we are all here."

Think about this. Paul and Silas were beaten up physically, just like you may find yourself beaten up spiritually today. But even in difficult circumstances Paul and Silas decided to worship—an act of gratitude unto God. They didn't complain or murmur or let the devil put words into their mouths: "Why me, Lord? Why am I going through this? Where are You, Lord? Where's my victory?" No; they worshipped and praised the Lord.

I want you to catch this: Paul and Silas' worship affected everyone in the prison. The prisoners stopped and listened from their place of despair. Men whom life had beaten down to nothing found themselves in a dark place in a prison cell—and it wasn't like today's prisons with three meals a day, free cable, a nice bed, and showers. This was a dungeon, a hole in the wall, a place of darkness.

Paul and Silas worshipped at the most inconvenient hour, at midnight. It was just like the man who knocked on his friend's door in the story from Luke 11. Paul and Silas didn't worry about the time. They just worshipped.

When you find yourself in a place where you feel empty— where you are in despair like the psalmist, your soul crying out in weariness—where do you run? I'm not talking about just being tired. This is not something you can come back from by taking a nap, taking some vitamins, or having an energy drink. Weariness of soul is when the devil plunges his weapons into you and leaves you bleeding spiritually, and you have nothing left to give.

When you are overcome by weariness of soul, where do you run? We tend to run to pastors and leaders, to conferences and events, and even to false prophets, but we bypass God. There is nothing wrong with going to a good conference, a good event, or a genuine pastor or leader. That's all good. But do you know what? Those are never first on my list. I run to Jesus. The only person who can give you what you need is the Lord Himself. Your healing and deliverance are in His hands.

The man who prays will accomplish more in a year than others will in a lifetime. Remember Luke 11:9 says, "So I say to you, ask, and it will be given to you; seek, and you will find; knock, and it will be opened to you" (NKJV). God promises us these blessings, but the devil is in his kingdom laughing and daring you to believe it in faith. Who are you going to obey?

F. B. Meyer said it like this: "The greatest tragedy in life is not unanswered prayer, but unoffered prayer."[2] When we look to other people for guidance but don't pray, it brings delay and allows the enemy to trap us.

It's time for you to start knocking. Be persistent and determined—more persistent and more determined than the devil. That's how we win our battles. The woman with the issue of blood had no strength in her body. She had gone to every medical doctor in her time. Not only was she drained physically, spiritually, emotionally, and mentally, but her bank account was drained too. She lived in a society where women didn't mean anything; they were second-class citizens. She had no hope. She didn't see tomorrow. She didn't see any healing. But then she heard a name.

She heard about Jesus, someone who had everything to give, just like the man in Luke 11. This precious woman pressed in with everything she had through the crowd, the sea of men surrounding Jesus. She didn't have a victim mentality. She didn't have a defeated mentality. She didn't say, "Why me?" or "Look at what the devil is doing to me." She only said to herself, "If I can touch His garment, I'll be healed." (See Luke 8:43–48.)

It's time for you to get up just like that woman and press and push and crawl to the other side, to victory. Let that be your story. It's not what you don't have; it's not what you need; it's who you have in front of you, the King of kings and the Lord of lords. Keep praying. Keep pressing. Let the devil know, "If you're going to be in my way, I'm going to run you over because I've got the prayers, I've got the anointing, and heaven has my bread. I still have the fight in me to win this battle."

IT'S NOT WHERE YOU START—IT'S WHERE YOU FINISH

There is a street fight scene in the movie *Rocky V*. Rocky had been knocked down and was bleeding, and his enemy was walking away. Then Rocky got up, called out his enemy's name, and said, "I didn't hear no bell. One more round."[3]

I think we should take those words spiritually and let the devil know, "I didn't hear no bell. One more round. Because greater is He who lives in me than he who lives in the world." (See 1 John 4:4.)

I want to share the powerful testimony of a precious man of God named William Cowper. He was born almost three hundred years ago. He was considered a great English poet in his time, but he became mentally unstable. His mother died when he was a young boy, and William was sent away to school. He struggled with depression, or what was called "melancholy" at the time, from then on.

When he was only thirty-two years old, like many of us today William found himself unable to deal with the things that were happening spiritually. He decided to commit suicide. The devil was up to something in his life, just like he is in your life today.

But God always has the last laugh, and together you will laugh in the devil's face.

First, William planned on poisoning himself with an overdose of opium. When that plan didn't work, he ordered a coach to take him to the Thames River, intending to throw himself into the water. He was going to jump off, but the water was too shallow, and there was a man sitting nearby "as if on purpose to prevent" the suicide. The following morning William took a penknife and tried to stab himself two or three times, but the tip of the blade was broken, and nothing happened. Then he tried to hang himself—three times in a row. His third attempt caused him to lose consciousness, but he ended up face down on the floor—and still alive.[4]

William was placed in an asylum for eighteen months. But God had a plan for him, just like He has a plan for you, and put him under a Christian doctor. Then, after William had spent months living in the asylum, one day God opened the windows of heaven, His pantry, and sent bread his way.

Near the window of William's room was a Bible. He opened up to Romans 3:25 (KJV): "Whom God hath set forth to be a propitiation through faith in his blood, to declare his righteousness for the remission of sins that are past, through the forbearance of God." Those words pierced his heart. He received strength to believe at that moment and received Christ as his Lord and Savior. He shook off his shame and started to feel free. The mercy of God set him free. He wrote, "Immediately I received strength to believe it, and the full beams of the Sun of Righteousness shone upon me....I could only look up to heaven... overwhelmed with love and wonder. But the work of the Holy Ghost is best described in his own words. It is 'joy unspeakable, and full of glory.'"[5]

The man was in a nuthouse, but he was filled with joy.

The devil was after this man because of the treasure inside him. The devil is after you for the same reason. He thinks he has you on the run, my brothers and sisters, but what a fool he is. As William Cowper wrote, "And Satan trembles, when he sees the weakest saint upon his knees."[6]

You can go to Jesus in your darkest hour. He has everything you need. As Thomas Keating said, the only way you can fail in prayer is not to show up.[7]

William Cowper later penned the beautiful words of a hymn people still sing today, "There Is a Fountain Filled with Blood":

> There is a fountain filled with blood
> Drawn from Immanuel's veins;
> And sinners, plunged beneath that flood,
> Lose all their guilty stains:
> Lose all their guilty stains,
> Lose all their guilty stains;
> And sinners, plunged beneath that flood,
> Lose all their guilty stains.
>
> The dying thief rejoiced to see
> That fountain in his day;
> And there may I, though vile as he,
> Wash all my sins away:
> Wash all my sins away,
> Wash all my sins away;
> And there may I, though vile as he,
> Wash all my sins away.[8]

This was part of the treasure inside that man. The devil tried to kill it—but God.

Let me share a spiritual nugget with you. I think we miss God's best because by the time we see the enemy, we've already put a name on him and it's too late. You need to cast the devil out before he even sets foot on the battlefield so that you can have the upper hand on him. Don't let the devil steal your victory.

Isaiah 40:29–31 says, "He gives strength to the weary, and to the one who lacks might He increases power. Though youths grow weary and tired, and vigorous young men stumble badly, yet those who wait for the LORD will gain new strength; they will mount up with wings like eagles, they will run and not get tired, they will walk and not become weary" (NASB). The word *weary* is mentioned three times in this scripture. Like I said before, this is not "I need a nap" weariness; it's weariness of the soul.

The amazing thing is that the end result in this scripture isn't weariness. It's the opposite. The key is to wait upon the Lord. He gives you strength. Quiet your soul. The devil uses the weapons of anxiety, uncertainty, and emptiness to make your soul weary; they bring you down to nothing. But here is the good news: "Those who wait for the LORD will gain new strength; they will mount up with wings like eagles, they will run and not get tired, they will walk and not become weary" (Isa. 40:31, NASB).

Psalm 3 says:

> LORD, how many are my foes! How many rise up against me! Many are saying of me, "God will not deliver him." But you, LORD, are a shield around me, my glory, the One who lifts my head high. I call out to the LORD, and he answers me from his holy mountain. I lie down and sleep; I wake again, because the LORD sustains me. I will not fear though tens of thousands assail me on every side. Arise, LORD! Deliver me, my God! Strike all my enemies on the jaw; break the teeth of the wicked. From the LORD comes deliverance. May your blessing be on your people.

This is how we stand on the side of victory in every season that God ordained for us before the foundations of the earth. He is our shield. He is the One who lifts our heads. He answers when we call. He delivers us.

Now pray these prayers with me to refresh and heal your soul and get back to God's perfect will, in Jesus' mighty name.

I thank You, Father God, for the blessings and the provision of the blood of Jesus.

I stand on the ground of the blood of Jesus to proclaim victory over spiritual weariness and depletion in my life, in the name of Jesus.

Let all demonic, satanic assignments that are trying to paralyze me and steal my spiritual strength and deplete my anointing in this battle, this fight, and this war shrivel up and die in the blood of Jesus.

Let the blood of my Lord and Savior Jesus Christ revive me and reenergize me from the crown of my head to the soles of my feet, in Jesus' mighty name.

I apply the blood of Jesus to every area of my life, completely and fully, this year, from the beginning to the end and everything in the middle, so that no weapon, no devil, no witch or warlock, and no satanic force will be able to accomplish any demonic assignment that they tailor-made, custom-made, or demonically engineered against me. Let them drown in the blood of Jesus. Amen.

I speak, by the anointing of the Holy Spirit, spiritual strength, power, and might in the anointing from the top of my head to the soles of my feet. May the blood of Jesus Christ cover me, my family, my loved ones, my ministry, my purpose, and my destiny, in Jesus' unmatchable, almighty name.

Let the blood of Jesus quicken all that is dead and lukewarm within me, in the name of Jesus Christ forevermore.

Chapter 6

FAITH IN DARK TIMES

EBREWS 11:6 TELLS us, "And without faith it is impossible to please God, because anyone who comes to him must believe that he exists and that he rewards those who earnestly seek him." Some people believe that fighting the enemy of our souls is done by words only. I often hear believers say, "I've got faith," "I bind you, Satan," "The Lord rebukes you, devil," and "I rebuke you, devil." Then we go down the list of rebuking, binding, and loosing—but nothing happens.

I know many of us say we have faith, but other religions out there have faith too, and nothing really happens for them. What the devil fears, what the devil worries about, is your prayer life. The devil doesn't want you to have a prayer life and a relationship with the Lord Jesus Christ because if you have those and faith, the devil doesn't stand a chance in hell against you in spiritual warfare in any season.

I hear many Christians say, "I have faith," "I believe God," or "I'm standing on faith," but I never hear anyone say, "I'm standing in the knowledge of God." Let's dive in deeper in this chapter to expose the devil's playbook.

Don't Let the Dark Times Determine Your Future

Remember the story about Paul and Silas we talked about earlier? They were beaten and thrown in jail, but they chose to worship God even in a dark prison in the dark of night. But there is more to that story.

Paul and Silas had been thrown in prison because God used them to set a girl with a demonic spirit, whose masters were profiting off her, free from bondage. Jesus Christ set her free through the hands of Paul and Silas. The key point that I want to show you about this story is that it doesn't matter if you're fighting the good fight, praying for your family and loved ones to be set free, standing for truth in the marketplace or your workplace, or standing for truth in the world today; the enemy has targeted you, and you may find yourself in dark times.

Paul and Silas were struck with many physical blows. The enemy has struck you with many spiritual blows, and you may find yourself in your midnight hour, in dark times, like Paul and Silas did. But notice the hearts of those two men of God. The Bible says they began "praying and singing hymns to God" (Acts 16:25, NKJV). Look what came out of their mouths. Look what came out of their hearts after they were struck with many blows and put into the deepest part of the prison. You might find yourself in the prison, the dark place, today, and the devil has struck you with many spiritual blows. What's coming out of your mouth? What's coming out of your heart?

The key to Paul and Silas' victory was that they sang and praised the Lord. When they did that, the foundations of the prison were shaken. The Bible says that "everyone's chains were loosed" (v. 26, NKJV). God sent an earthquake, chains fell off, and doors were opened.

That is going to be your victory today. Chains are going to

fall off, and doors are going to open. I'm going to show you how to get there. I'm going to teach you more about how the devil's playbook works.

Look at Paul and Silas. In the midnight hour, in the dark place, after they had been struck with many blows, they knew one thing. You probably think you know what I'm talking about; you might say they had faith. Yes, they did—but it was bigger than that. It was more than that. A lot of us have faith, but it's hollow. It's empty. We have faith, but it has question marks. We have faith, but we also have doubts and unbelief.

Paul and Silas had faith that wasn't hollow, empty, or doubtful. They had a song in their hearts. They praised and talked to God, and God sent them an earthquake. God wants to send a spiritual earthquake your way today to set you free, once and for all.

TAKE YOUR FAITH TO THE SPIRITUAL GYM

The disciples walked with Jesus for three years. Put the story of the disciples opposite the story we just read about Paul and Silas. God rebuked the disciples four times, in four different places, for having little faith.

I know what you're going to say: "Well, the Bible says that if you have faith the size of a mustard seed, you can move a mountain." That is true; if your faith has substance behind it, you can move any mountain and cast it into any sea. But in this story the disciples' "little" faith was worn down, lukewarm, anemic, and depleted. Their little faith had question marks, doubt, and fear. That's why Jesus rebuked them.

Matthew 6:30 (NASB) says, "But if God so clothes the grass of the field, which is alive today and tomorrow is thrown into the furnace, will He not much more clothe you? You of little faith!" That was the first time Jesus rebuked the disciples.

This is what God had to say about them next:

> When He got into the boat, His disciples followed Him. And behold, a violent storm developed on the sea, so that the boat was being covered by the waves; but Jesus Himself was asleep. And they came to Him and woke Him, saying, "Save us, Lord; we are perishing!" He said to them, "Why are you afraid, you men of little faith?" Then He got up and rebuked the winds and the sea, and it became perfectly calm. The men were amazed, and said, "What kind of a man is this, that even the winds and the sea obey Him?"
>
> —Matthew 8:23–27, nasb

Jesus rebuked them a third time:

> When the disciples saw Him walking on the sea, they were terrified, and said, "It is a ghost!" And they cried out in fear. But immediately Jesus spoke to them, saying, "Take courage, it is I; do not be afraid."
>
> Peter responded and said to Him, "Lord, if it is You, command me to come to You on the water." And He said, "Come!" And Peter got out of the boat and walked on the water, and came toward Jesus. But seeing the wind, he became frightened, and when he began to sink, he cried out, saying, "Lord, save me!" Immediately Jesus reached out with His hand and took hold of him, and said to him, "You of little faith, why did you doubt?"
>
> —Matthew 14:26–31, nasb

Then Jesus rebuked the disciples a fourth time:

> But Jesus, aware of this, said, "You men of little faith, why are you discussing among yourselves the fact that you have no bread? Do you not yet understand nor remember the

five loaves of the five thousand, and how many baskets you picked up? Nor the seven loaves of the four thousand, and how many large baskets you picked up? How is it that you do not understand that I did not speak to you about bread? But beware of the leaven of the Pharisees and Sadducees." Then they understood that He did not say to beware of the leaven of bread, but of the teaching of the Pharisees and Sadducees.

—MATTHEW 16:8–12, NASB

It's amazing that the disciples were rebuked four times. The first time they were rebuked because they didn't trust God for provision. The second time they were rebuked for fear and anxiety. The third time they were rebuked for not trusting God fully. And the fourth rebuke was for mishandling what Jesus had told them. These are the kinds of subtle attacks the devil uses on us today.

Paul and Silas took a different spiritual approach than the disciples did. They chose to be men of faith—and not the little, lukewarm kind of faith.

Having faith is knowing that God loves you, cares for you, and is a present help at all times. Faith knows God is able to keep you and move you forward. Faith knows there is breakthrough for every season of your life. You need faith to know God's voice and how He speaks so you can see the subtle attacks of the devil on any given day.

I think we play around with the idea of faith, just like a person who has a snake wrapped around him. We think it's cute and fine until the snake starts to wrap himself around us tightly, and then we start to scream and cry out. That's how subtle attacks of the enemy work. He starts to squeeze you, and your spiritual life gets serious quickly.

Little faith is cute, but it's not going to work in the dark times. Where we are today and where God is taking us, the days are dark and evil. The devil has upped his game, and the church is playing in the spiritual sandbox, in the baby pool. The church—including me and my brothers and sisters, at times—reminds me of the sons of Sceva. They had little faith to move little mountains. (See Acts 19:11–16.) Let me say it like this: in dark times, you need strong faith.

I once heard, "Faith is believing God in spite of appearances and obeying God in spite of consequences."[1] Let me give you the icing on the cake and crush the head of the devil. This is what we lack, and this is where we fall behind. We have one part of the story but don't know the other part, which the devil has been hiding and distracting us from. Paul and Silas knew it very well, though, because instead of complaining like the disciples did they began to praise and worship the Lord.

Let me give you the other part of the story, and let's put the devil to sleep: Faith is built on the knowledge of God. It isn't built on, "Oh, I believe those principles." That's what the devil wants you to act on. He wants you to fight him in that spiritual atmosphere. That's why we are in dark times. The devil is a liar.

Faith is built on the knowledge of God, our Lord and Savior. The devil isn't fighting you just because you believe. The devil is fighting you to keep you away from the knowledge of God—who God is, what His character is like, and what He can do. Even the demons have the knowledge of God—and they tremble, the Bible says (Jas. 2:19).

What about us? It's like the Bible says: "Faith without works is dead" (Jas. 2:26, NASB). Faith without the knowledge of God is dead. That's why the devil wants you to hold on to faith with no knowledge of God. Hosea 4:6 (NASB) says, "My people are destroyed for lack of knowledge. Since you have rejected knowledge, I also will reject you from being My priest. Since you have forgotten the Law of your God, I also will forget your children."

The devil doesn't mind if you go to church. The devil doesn't mind if you read your Bible as a religious person, keeping your spirit empty because you have no knowledge of God. That's little faith. Great faith has a great God. Little faith has a little God.

A lot of us today want the recipe for how to fight in dark times, but we don't want to build our faith on the foundation of the knowledge of God because we're too busy. We're too distracted and preoccupied. We're like the people who want the blessings of the Lord but don't want Him. Do you want to build your house? Build it on the rock of the knowledge of God—the knowledge of His character, who He is, and what He can do.

When we have little faith, we are missing out. Paul and Silas knew that if they worshipped and praised God, not complaining even though they were struck with many blows, God would send an earthquake to shake the foundations of the prison. Chains fell off and doors were opened. That's what the devil fears the most.

Today, the devil is defeated. It doesn't matter that he has a playbook. He is now demolished because we know how he attacks. We're going to live in the knowledge of God. We are going to have great faith because we have a great God.

DROPPING THE BOMB ON THE ENEMY'S CAMP

In 1 Peter and 2 Peter, the apostle Peter spoke into the lives of precious brothers and sisters who were living in dark times. They were being hunted and killed for their faith. The devil is not afraid of you when you just have faith, but when you also have the knowledge of God, the enemy trembles. Second Peter 3:18 (NASB) says, "But grow in the grace and knowledge of our

Lord and Savior Jesus Christ. To Him be the glory, both now and to the day of eternity. Amen."

Peter gave you a weapon of mass destruction to use against the devil. He told you how to drop a bomb on the enemy's camp. He was speaking to brothers and sisters who didn't even know if they would see tomorrow because of their faith, because of their relationship with the Lord Jesus Christ. Look what Jesus said through the words of Peter: "Grow in the grace and knowledge of our Lord and Savior Jesus Christ." The devil has been trying to hide this from you. Don't read through it and miss this part. This will cause mass destruction against the devil and his playbook.

Underline *grace and knowledge* in your Bible. Grow in the grace and knowledge of God. That's how we fight the good fight. It's not yelling faith. Stop rebuking the devil with empty words. You sound like the sons of Sceva; the real fight shows up, and you have nothing to fight with. In dark times, instead of us having the devil on the run, he has us on the run.

Victory comes on the heels of the grace and knowledge of God. That's where the foundation of faith lives. The devil has been hiding this from the church for quite a while, but we are waking up. It's time for us to decide whether we will grow up or die a spiritual death on the battlefield.

Stop listening to dead pastors and leaders. Listen instead to the story of Jesus in the wilderness. Matthew 4:1 (NASB) says, "Then Jesus was led up by the Spirit into the wilderness to be tempted by the devil." Jesus didn't confront Julio. He didn't confront Fred or Crazy Willie or Crazy Daisy or Wanda. He confronted the devil himself. This was no principality, demon, or python. This was no Jezebel spirit. Satan himself showed up for the fight.

If Jesus would have said, "Oh, devil. Boom! Bang! Satan, you are done," do you think He would have overcome the three temptations? Absolutely not. The only way the devil would have died was laughing. But Jesus said, "It is written." He was talking to the devil about the knowledge of God, about His Word and His character.

The devil didn't stand a chance and left the battlefield. Stop practicing that "Boom! Bang! I bind you, Satan. Get behind me" theology with no foundation in the knowledge of God. First Corinthians 13:11 (NASB) says, "When I was a child, I used to speak like a child, think like a child, reason like a child; when I became a man, I did away with childish things." Again, it's time for us to grow up. Peter made it clear that we need to grow in the grace and knowledge of God.

GET TO KNOW KING JESUS, AND NEVER FORGET HIM

Every battle you face is a test of your faith and your knowledge of God. The devil doesn't want you to know that, because if you do, and you live in the knowledge of God, then your faith will be strong. You have strong faith in a strong God, great faith in a great God. It's time to tell the devil and his kingdom they are toast. Let me say it again. Every battle you face is a test of faith, and every test of your faith is a challenge to get to know how big God is.

The devil has a new thing going on today, and we're eating it up. He is using a new weapon right in our faces. We think it's cute, and no one is addressing it. No one is talking about it. I don't care; I'm going to say it like it is because I live by the truth of God and not the opinions of people. Many of us—thank God not all of us—are deconstructing our faith. How demonic, how diabolical that is. Deconstructing your faith means to deconstruct the knowledge of God in your life so the devil can eat you for lunch. It's the most demonic, despicable thing happening today in the church around the world. It is satanically engineered; the devil understands that believers are waking up, so he has to fight double overtime, sometimes triple or quadruple overtime, to try to get victory over our lives.

What if I said, "Well, I want Jesus, but don't put the Holy Spirit in me"? What a joke! How demonic would that be? Really? You're going to deconstruct your faith because the devil is telling you to do so? You're deconstructing the knowledge of God in your life? Pastors and leaders are nothing but a joke when they buy into this thing, this idea of deconstruction of faith. It is total hogwash.

We are losing the battle for our souls. The concept of deconstructing our faith is another scheme straight out of the devil's playbook. We're really exposing the devil in this chapter. We're giving him a beatdown. If you catch this in your spirit, it's completely over for the devil, his playbook, his kingdom, and his cronies.

We're building the church today asking people to get to know who they are instead of who God is. If you go into a church that makes it about you—knowing who you are; discovering yourself, your gifts, and what kind of anointing you have—instead of about knowing God and growing in the grace and knowledge of Him, run for the hills. If nothing is said about who God is in the house of God, then it is the house of Satan, not the house of Jesus Christ. Those leaders are deconstructing your faith. And they aren't stopping there. They want to make you the main focus, delivering messages about how to be a better you, seven steps to this, twelve steps to that, while saying nothing about God. This is the devil at his best. This is demonic. It's time for us to turn and repent.

I don't care about me; I care to know God. I don't lift up my hands because I'm worthy; I lift up my hands because He's worthy. I don't need to know seven steps about me. I need to know about God. If I know Him, then I will know who I am in Him.

Knowing who you are alone is not good enough. It's not going to lead you to victory on the battlefield or in the dark times. I built my faith on the knowledge of Jesus Christ. I honor God, not me. I wasn't meant to be somebody; I was meant to know Him. I was created to know Him. The reason I read the Bible is to grow in the knowledge of Him. I worship God, talk to Jesus, and attend a real church—that makes me a winner in Him.

This focus on self comes straight out of the devil's playbook. When the church is preaching about you and about deconstructing your faith instead of reading the Bible and preaching about the knowledge of God to help you grow strong in your faith, it's coming right out of the devil's playbook. Don't even get me started on another concept straight from his playbook: people getting "debaptized." People are lining up to debaptize themselves like they line up at Starbucks. We need to know Jesus so the devil can't use his playbook to kill, steal, and destroy us.

I find my strength in the Lord Jesus Christ. Knowing Him is how we fight our battles. I don't need to discover me; I only need to know Him. But knowing Him takes time. Growing in the knowledge of God takes time. That's why the devil tries to steal your time. The Bible talks about "making the most of your time, because the days are evil" (Eph. 5:16, NASB). Other translations say "redeeming the time" (e.g., NKJV). When the Bible talks about redeeming or making the most of your time, it's not because you're late for work or you're late to get a donut or coffee. It's about making time for church, the Bible, prayer, and worship.

The devil is also trying to steal our Bibles because we find wisdom and the knowledge of our Lord and Savior in the precious, priceless pages—and that's where faith grows. That's where we get our spiritual substance.

Let me wrap it up for you in a bow. Growing in the knowledge of God is like attending spiritual boot camp to equip you for the battle in dark times. Dark times aren't just coming; they're already here. The devil knows when your faith and your knowledge of God are being tested. Do you know it?

Listen to the words of Jesus in Luke 22:31–32: "Simon, Simon, Satan has asked to sift all of you as wheat. But I have prayed for you, Simon, that your faith may not fail. And when you have turned back, strengthen your brothers." What an amazing moment in Scripture. Jesus was telling Peter, "I have allowed and given permission for you to go into the battlefield. Take faith with you because you're going to be sifted like wheat. But I'm praying for you. I'm not praying for your battlefield or for you to beat up Satan. I'm praying that your faith will not fail."

Hear the words of Jesus. He could have said, "I'm praying for you so you can win in round three," or, "I'm praying for you so you can crush the devil in the first round." No, no. Jesus said He was praying that Peter's faith wouldn't fail. In other words, "The knowledge of Me inside of you will come into agreement with your faith, and the devil will regret asking My permission to allow you to go into the battlefield."

Foolish Entrapment of the Enemy

Let me give you another key to victory. The purpose of every demonic strategy is to twist and distort who God is. This is in the devil's playbook. It's a lie from the pit of hell. The devil has you distracted, chasing things that are secondary: "I'm chasing the anointing." "I'm chasing my purpose and my destiny so God can make me an influential preacher." You're chasing influence and you're chasing gifts, but you have no knowledge of God, which produces fruit. The Bible says, "Many will say to me on that day, 'Lord, Lord, did we not prophesy in your name and in your name drive out demons and in your name perform many miracles?' Then I will tell them plainly, 'I never knew you. Away from me, you evildoers!'" (Matt. 7:22–23).

The devil tries to distort and twist your faith and turn it upside down. It's amazing that the people in this passage of Scripture claimed they were casting out demons and doing the work of the Lord, but God basically said to them, "Depart from Me; you have no knowledge of Me and no fruit, so I never knew you." In other words, they were influencers who operated in the gifts but did not operate in the knowledge of God, so they had no fruit. It was a bad day for them, having been ordered to depart from the presence of our holy God.

Remember, even if we have knowledge of God in our spirits and in our hearts, the devil will try to twist and distort it on the battlefield. That's where the fight is; that's where faith and the knowledge of God crush the head of the serpent—on any battle-field, in any season, in any given time. When knowledge and faith walk together, the devil doesn't stand a chance.

C. S. Lewis fought with that kind of faith, a faith built on the knowledge of God. Lewis was an amazing man of God. He married a precious woman of God named Joy Davidman. Soon after, she was diagnosed with cancer and died. Lewis kept a journal during that time, which was published as a book called *A Grief Observed*. It tells the story of his grief and his struggle after his wife died right in front of his eyes. It was a raw moment for his faith. The pages of his journal talk about how he perceived

God in the battlefield of his mind while he watched his wife die. Remember, every battle is a faith fight, and every faith fight is a chapter in the knowledge of God.

This was the challenge C. S. Lewis faced. Listen to these words he wrote during the dark times of his faith fight: "Not that I am (I think) in much danger of ceasing to believe in God. The real danger is of coming to believe such dreadful things about Him."[2] That kind of thing comes straight out of the devil's playbook. It's not that we stop believing who God is, but we begin to believe dreadful, ugly things about Him.

Today you may find yourself in that place where you think dreadful things about who God is. C. S. Lewis wrote, "The conclusion I dread is not 'So there's no God after all,' but 'So this is what God's really like. Deceive yourself no longer.'"[3] In other words, Lewis was saying the real danger isn't not believing in God or giving up belief in God, but instead believing that He could be so cruel as to kill his wife. Lewis was afraid he might come to the conclusion that there is a God, but He is really cruel.

Those were C. S. Lewis' thoughts during his darkest time. The devil was pounding on his faith and his mind. Many of us today feel the same emotions and feelings that our precious brother felt in his darkest hour. And we know God is OK with that because He said in His Word, "Come now, and let us reason together" (Isa. 1:18, NKJV).

But look at the end of C. S. Lewis' story, the beautiful words he painted on paper because he didn't stay in the dark place, in that state of hopelessness. He said that despite his grief, he could still enjoy God by praising Him, and "I need Christ, not something that resembles Him."[4] What powerful words from this precious man's heart. That should be our story too.

I have good news for you: No matter where you find yourself

in the fight on the battlefield, victory is yours. The devil has already lost. Let me tell you an amazing story I heard about a painting of the devil called *Checkmate*.

One day a grand master of chess saw the painting. The grand master took his time staring at the chess board in the painting. Doing so, he noticed something shocking: the normal interpretation of the painting (that the devil had the man in checkmate) was incorrect. Though the devil seemed to be the obvious champion, it turned out he was not winning after all. The man who thought he was losing was actually winning. According to the way the pieces were arranged on the chessboard, the man's king had one more move.[5]

Listen to the story, my brothers and sisters. The battlefield is a chessboard. We might move a few pieces, but with the King—His name is Jesus—we always have one more move. It's called the knowledge of God. It's wrapped in faith. We can tell the devil "Checkmate" on the chessboard of our battlefield and put him to sleep once and for all because we live on the victory side of the cross. It starts there and it ends there. To God be the glory forever and ever, amen.

Chapter 7

TAKING THE VEIL OFF THE DEMONIC

I WANT TO SHARE something with you. I want to bring you back into a world that not even Hollywood could explain. I want to bring you back to a place and describe it so you understand what spiritual warfare is really all about. My life seems to be unique and very different, but it's not better than anyone else's. I count myself to be the least of anyone God has saved. I'm OK with that. I'm in good company with the apostle Paul.

It's amazing how Paul was recruited in the third heaven when he heard the voice of Jesus Christ in Acts 9:4–5:

> He fell to the ground and heard a voice say to him, "Saul, Saul, why do you persecute me?"
> "Who are you, Lord?" Saul asked.
> "I am Jesus, whom you are persecuting," he replied.

What a moment for a man who was a monster, religious, intellectual, and dangerous all at the same time. The idea that God would speak to him out of all the people in his time is amazing. I believe it was a heart issue. God knew He could penetrate this man's heart. My story is similar to the apostle Paul's.

We hear powerful testimonies of people who have been delivered from the occult, and I rejoice for every single one of them. I'm so blessed and grateful to the Lord Jesus Christ for touching their hearts and bringing them out and to the foot of the cross. Today many people dabble in, participate in, interact with, or even pledge their allegiance to the occult, including many people in Hollywood. Some do it for music contracts or movie contracts. When you pledge yourself to the occult on that level, you're telling the devil, "If you give me this, I will sell you my time." We know for a fact, 100 percent, that unless that person is touched by Jesus Christ, they will spend eternity separated from God. They're selling their time to the devil, saying, "I serve you, I'm faithful to you, and I will follow you."

RIPPING OFF THE SPIRITUAL CURTAIN

The reason I share this testimony is not because of me. It's because when God steps into your world, when He steps into time and knows your address, it becomes a powerful testimony of His mercy, His grace, and His goodness. That was my story.

Like many Christians today, I was born into the occult. The bloodline on my father's side included witches and warlocks and carried satanic practices and ceremonies, dedications, rituals from blood sacrifices, cutting, animal sacrifices, and demonic ceremonies with demons, principalities, water spirits, marine spirits, and the mocking spirits in what we call the high places. My bloodline even had astral projection of devils and those from the first and second heavens. That is the place where I was recruited from—the second heaven.

One warm, sunny summer day back when I was an innocent young boy, I was playing in a vacant lot where a building once stood. The building had been demolished, and the lot was my playground. I went there with one of my crazy bully friends from the neighborhood to throw rocks at empty buildings to break windows, trying to see who could throw the farthest. It was far from Disney World and Great Adventure, but that's how we had fun.

Suddenly a satanic, demonic necklace from the second heaven fell at my feet. It was called the seven demonic powers, from the satanic kingdom of the devil. I stuffed the necklace into my pocket before my friend could blink. Then I heard my mother's voice calling my name. I panicked and told my friend, "My mom just called me. I gotta go." It wasn't my mom calling me; it was a demon. That's when I was introduced to a familial spirit, at the age of seven.

When I was eight years old, one day my mom and I went with my auntie, who was the head witch of the bloodline curse in my dad's family bloodline, to the house of a close friend of hers—a witch, medium, and satanic devil worshipper—to get tarot cards read for my mom and my aunt. In the demonic world this is called a report card and assesses your demonic allegiance, ceremonies, and other demonic spiritual updates as you walk with the devil hand in hand.

When we got to the place, it was a very gloomy, dingy apartment with outdated furniture, faded walls, and black floors. It was supposed to be my aunt and my mom getting their cards read, but the witch and the devil had a different plan. They fixed their eyes on me, and my world was never the same. I was not just recruited, but I was initiated into the dark side through open doors in my family's bloodline curse. A week later I participated in my first ceremony. I was going to demon church, dealing with the masters and the hierarchy of the witchcraft world, and being trained, discipled, and equipped to walk the walk.

Fast-forward many years, and I got married on Halloween. It was a demonic initiation beyond human comprehension. That night we heard the cries of the animals as they were being slaughtered. Warlocks and witches came to satanically baptize my wedding. I became the third-highest-ranking devil worshipper from New York City to Miami to Haiti. I made contracts, and ceremonies and rituals were performed on my body with cuttings and shed blood by the devil and the demonic forces of his kingdom—more than a human being can handle. The highest devil worshipper on the planet carved twenty-one roads of the dark side into the flesh on the right side of my shoulder.

I knew the voice of every demon, every principality. I knew the voices of marine and water spirits. I was trained to know the voices of demonic spirits and all their names, colors, when they were born, where they were born geographically in this world, and so on. But it was all a lie. The demons—angels that fell from heaven—were not born. They were created. Humanity is born.

The demons adopted identities. They adopted names. They adopted geographical locations in the satanic world. A demon that was an angel in heaven lost his post in heaven because Lucifer, whom now we call Satan, was an influencer and a tempter. That's how his ministry started. He was cast down to the earth.

> How you have fallen from heaven, morning star, son of the dawn! You have been cast down to the earth, you who once laid low the nations! You said in your heart, "I will ascend to the heavens; I will raise my throne above the stars of God; I will sit enthroned on the mount of assembly, on the utmost heights of Mount Zaphon. I will ascend above the tops of the clouds; I will make myself like the Most High." But you are brought down to the realm of the dead, to the depths of the pit.
>
> —Isaiah 14:12–15

This is Lucifer's heart: black, filthy, and dirty. This is his corrupt mindset. In Luke 10:18 Jesus said, "I saw Satan fall like lightning from heaven." It was Satan's downfall. He fell from grace.

I remember like it was yesterday when as a young believer in Jesus, I felt obligated to go to the most satanic meeting that a human being could comprehend. Seventeen high-level warlocks and a few witches of high rank in the satanic world attended the meeting. I didn't go because I wanted to be there. I was still perplexed, torn between two worlds, the world of light and the world of darkness. I was falling in love with Jesus Christ, but I felt obligated—I guess you would call it a commitment—to the satanic world. I still had demonic residue in my life.

I attended the meeting. At midnight the devil showed up, and the participants allowed the enemy, the devil himself, to use their bodies. He turned to me as I was sitting there. My body was there, but my heart wasn't. He asked me, "My son, can I share something with you in a demonic language?"

I said, "Sure you can."

"You know why God threw us out of heaven?"

I looked at him and said, "I have no idea. Why?"

He said, "Because he was jealous of us."

That night, because the devil didn't get the response he wanted—my cheering him on and acting like I used to, excited and jumping out of my skin—he left so upset with me that if he could have taken my life that night, he would have done it at the drop of a hat.

It was four in the morning when I left the meeting. It was so cold, probably about fifteen or twenty degrees, that I could see the breath coming out of my mouth. I didn't have a car, so the other warlocks said, "Hey, John, get in the car. Come on. We'll take you home. It's freezing out here. We're done with the meeting."

I put my hoodie over my head, shrugged my shoulders, and said, "It's OK. I'm gonna walk home."

As I started to walk the empty streets toward home, I felt the presence of the Holy Spirit walking with me under the streetlights on that cold winter morning in the Bronx. I felt like a little boy with a good Father walking me home from school. What a moment and what a blessing that was. I made it home safely and never went back to another meeting ever again.

I'm a Demon; I Have No Name

I want to share a heartfelt moment with you about spiritual warfare. It's amazing.

> They went across the lake to the region of the Gerasenes. When Jesus got out of the boat, a man with an impure spirit came from the tombs to meet him. This man lived in the tombs, and no one could bind him anymore, not even with a chain. For he had often been chained hand and foot, but he tore the chains apart and broke the irons on his feet. No one was strong enough to subdue him. Night and day among the tombs and in the hills he would cry out and cut himself with stones.
>
> When he saw Jesus from a distance, he ran and fell on his knees in front of him. He shouted at the top of his voice, "What do you want with me, Jesus, Son of the Most High God? In God's name don't torture me!" For Jesus had said to him, "Come out of this man, you impure spirit!"
>
> Then Jesus asked him, "What is your name?"
>
> "My name is Legion," he replied, "for we are many." And he begged Jesus again and again not to send them out of the area.
>
> —MARK 5:1–10

There were territorial spirits inside of this man. It's interesting to see that our Lord Jesus Christ, our Savior, spoke to the demons because this man couldn't speak for himself. The man had lost his identity; he had lost his character; he had lost who he was as a person. The demons spoke on his behalf.

I want to shed light on this. Jesus asked the demons their names. Think about it. They all could have said, "My name is Julio. My name is Fred. My name is Willie. My name is Wanda. My name is Daisy." They all could have just said their names. But no, their response to Jesus was about their identity. "Legion" was not the name they had in heaven. A legion was a military unit of the Roman Empire made up of two thousand to six thousand soldiers. When the demons answered that their name was Legion, they were trying to intimidate Jesus Christ by saying, "We are many, and You are by Yourself."

Jesus wasn't intimidated, though. He showed us at that moment that He is God and He is all-powerful. If He can cast out one demon, He can cast out thousands.

Demons operate under identities, not names. They take up names to communicate with you, to connect with you so you can understand and have a bridge between the real world and the demonic world. Jesus easily could have said, "Your name is this. Your name is that. This person is in there. That person is in there." He could have called each demon out by name, all two thousand of them, one by one at the drop of a hat because Jesus is God.

Jesus was addressing the identity of the demon that plagued this man. Demonic forces had stolen the man's identity. It's like when we say *infirmity*, we're describing the condition of the person. When we say *tormenting spirits*, we're describing the action and condition of the person. When we say *homosexual spirit,* we're describing the condition of a false identity in a person because the demon itself is not homosexual. The demon is a foul spirit.

Because demons were fallen angels in heaven with Lucifer, they don't have names. They probably did have names when they were in heaven, but Jesus never disclosed the actual names of the angels that fell, other than Lucifer. The only other angel names that have been revealed to us as believers are Michael and Gabriel.

In the spiritual warfare world, when we fight for deliverance, when we fight to set people free at conferences and events or when we do personal deliverance one on one, we're dealing with identities of demonic forces that are plaguing, incarcerating, tormenting, inflicting, and hijacking people by stealing their true identities. The Book of Job says, "So Satan went out from the presence of the LORD and afflicted Job with painful sores from the soles of his feet to the crown of his head" (2:7). Satan himself afflicted Job. The Bible didn't call it an infirmity spirit or a python spirit or a Jezebel spirit. The devil did not call himself an infirmity spirit. The devil inflicted upon Job what the devil wanted to execute on him spiritually and physically: sickness.

When people experience sickness and go to the doctor's office, but the doctor can't put his or her finger on the condition, we know it's an infirmity. But what is its identity? What is the root issue? The doctor will ask questions to get to the root of the sickness or condition and identify why the person is sitting in the office feeling that way: "How long have you been feeling this way? Is this something that runs in your family?" The point I'm trying to convey is we need to deal with the identity of what the demon is bringing to the battle. It's not just "Come out, Python. Come out, Jezebel. Come out, marine spirit." It's more than that.

We need to get to the root and the identity of the demonic attack so we can shut the door on it once and for all.

Marine spirits own the oceans and rivers—or so they think. When I was into the demonic world, the demons wanted us to visit rivers and oceans and cemeteries to perform contract ceremonies and rituals. A marine spirit is a demon that uses the ocean as a point of reference to incarcerate people by having them partake in rituals of the ocean. They use it as an open door to gain legal rights over you. But the devil doesn't live there. He visits and uses those places, but he doesn't live there. So instead of chasing after names, I chase after the root of whatever is afflicting my brother or sister. That is how you engage in spiritual warfare and destroy the attacks in a person's life.

The root of the demonic, satanic attack, the identity of it, is what we need to confront so we can hit it head-on by the power of the Holy Spirit. Remember, demons, devils, and principalities don't have names. They have identities that they use—like homosexuality, for example. A demon is not a homosexual. He messes with your identity. The demon steals your original identity like an identity thief and gives you a fake one so you have a false idea of what God created you to be. He plagues and afflicts you with that false identity and then makes you act out what you've been plagued with.

It's the same thing with pornography. When a man or woman is addicted to porn, he or she is afflicted by the spirits of lust and perversion, which are demonic identities from the kingdom of darkness and the devil's playbook.

Demons that operate in hospitals use infirmity attacks (in spiritual warfare and deliverance we call them "infirmity spirits" or "premature death spirits") on people to torment them and rob them of the healthy life that God created them to have. The same thing happens at asylums. Demons use these spirits of affliction to try to destroy you and your body because the enemy knows the body is the temple of the Holy Spirit. They use systems and methods to bring this demonic, satanic chaos into people's lives. We dress these spirits up with names like "infirmity," "premature death," and "sickness," but they are all methods that demons operate with to get their way.

The same is true with drug and alcohol addictions, gender confusion, abuse, and everything else the devil uses to steal, kill, and destroy. Because I lived in the demonic world for twenty-five years, I know the language, the behaviors, and the actions of devils, demons, and principalities. I know how they work. So I won't go and say, "Come out, Jezebel. Come out, Ahab. Come out, Julio." I'm going to deal with the root issue, whether it is a generational or bloodline curse or anything else.

Don't beat up the name. Beat up the identity of the demon, what's happening to the person being victimized by spiritual warfare, so the person can be set free through Jesus Christ and the power of the Holy Spirit. It's not about the demons' names. Stop chasing names. We have to battle more than a demon's name to set the captives free. Start destroying demonic identities by the power of the Holy Spirit. Smite those devils and bring the judgment of God upon their heads. Cast them out in Jesus' unmatchable name.

When I lived in the witchcraft world and I wanted to hurt or destroy someone, I would make a contract with a demon or principality to go after that person. I would come into agreement with the demon. Let's say, for example, I wanted to bring premature death on a person. The demon was not a premature death spirit. He would try to steal from, kill, and destroy that person before his time, using a car accident, a mugging, or some other violent act to accomplish the mission. He would use methods or systems; in other words, he would create a situation to end that person's life prematurely.

I hope you now understand why demons don't have names. They take up identities and use methods and demonic systems to accomplish their demonic agendas. Yes, we have names like "infirmity" to describe what's happening to a person in the spirit realm, but the demon's agenda is bigger than a name. So by the power of the Holy Spirit we destroy the satanic systems, operations, and methods, and that's how we get victory in Christ Jesus our Lord and Savior in the battle. I think I can get a hallelujah on that one.

I don't know why God allowed me to live in the demonic world for twenty-five years. But I know in my heart it's not where we start that's important; it's where we finish. I'm beyond blessed that He knew my name and rescued me from the demonic world and today I'm able to be an evangelist for Jesus Christ, a voice of the kingdom and a voice in Christianity to expose the devil's playbook at its core, at the root.

Many churches today don't teach, disciple, or equip the saints of God. I pray in the mighty name of Jesus that this chapter will be a blessing to you and you will become a soldier for Christ. It's time to be His body, His bride, and His army. We live for a kingdom that cannot be shaken or moved, a kingdom that cannot be altered or modified.

Heaven is our home, and earth is our battlefield. The devil doesn't have leverage over us. He doesn't have the upper hand against the body of Christ. We're the army, we're the bride, and we're the body. That's who we are. Now that you have the devil's playbook and know how demons play their games, go make Jesus Christ proud.

Chapter 8

MIRACLES AND TESTIMONIES

IT IS AN act of love when God shows up unannounced, unexpected, and often uninvited. Isaiah 55:8–9 (NKJV) says, "'For My thoughts are not your thoughts, nor are your ways My ways,' says the LORD. 'For as the heavens are higher than the earth, so are My ways higher than your ways, and My thoughts than your thoughts.'" God displays His majesty, power, and love to humanity. Whether it's a simple prayer, a cry from your heart, or a desperate plea, He hears every whisper that comes from your heart.

How amazing God is that He will step out of eternity and into time in order to write a beautiful story. The stories that are written when God shows up are called testimonies from heaven. Only God, our Lord Jesus Christ, and the power of the Holy Spirit, is able to write these amazing, powerful, beautiful testimonies. One of the beautiful things about God is that He doesn't show favoritism (Rom. 2:11). In other words, God doesn't think like we do. He can show up in any place at any time and write a testimony about you. That's how awesome He is, and that's how much He loves you. Don't you ever forget it—in Jesus' mighty name, amen.

I want to share some testimonies with you. Enjoy these blessings. One day you may be telling your own story, written by God

95

Himself, who holds the pen and writes the story of each of our lives.

TESTIMONY OF BROTHER VALIK ORGANYK FROM UKRAINE

The first time in my life I heard John Ramirez's testimony was in 2016, and I was delivered by John's YouTube prayer from demons choking me in dreams after I renounced tarot card readings. A reading had only been done one time in my life. I could sleep well after two years of choking in the night.

Two years ago I did some online Christian schools of other men of God. But the Lord didn't allow me to join their ministries. I prayed three times, and then I decided to join Inner Circle just to try it.[1] As 2022 started, I joined Inner Circle. I did twenty-one days of fasting, and after two months, the war started in my country, Ukraine. The first day of the war, I posted in the Inner Circle Facebook group to pray for me, and Sister Eliza from New York and six other women started to pray for me and Ukraine.

Then on a Zoom call John Ramirez prayed for me and released the warring angels to protect my village. In my village unbelievers saw two huge angels standing above the village. I am alive, and my village is completely safe. Not even one house is damaged, yet in places as near as five to twenty miles away, there has been much destruction and death.

My life will never be the same after joining the Inner Circle and John's ministry. Thank you, Lord!

I am blessed by this. My ears and my heart rejoice over this testimony of the power of prayer. When we pray, we don't know the impact it has in the spirit realm. One person prayed, and the whole village was protected. Never underestimate your prayer life and what God is doing behind the scenes. What a testimony of God answering prayer, not only for Valik but for his family, his loved ones, and even his village. God is good. I rejoice and celebrate this incredible testimony with my awesome brother and the people in Ukraine.

Testimony of Heidi

When my daughter turned fourteen, I started noticing some pretty drastic changes. She started wanting her beautiful long [hair] cut super short, and she dyed it all different colors. She gouged her earlobes out. She would lie in her room for hours and hours alone.

When she turned fifteen, I received a call from the school principal telling me that my daughter requested to use the boys' bathroom and that she wanted to be called Alex.

My heart broke as I questioned her. She told me she was really a boy named Alex. She started binding herself to hide her femininity. She was in a dark place. Nothing I could say to her made it better. She wouldn't take showers for days on end, and no amount of begging and pleading would make her brush her teeth.

She self-harmed regularly. She would go into fits of rage and scream, or she wouldn't speak at all. My child was lost in darkness, and I had no way of getting to her.

I was not much better. I struggled with suicidal thoughts and depression so much that some days I could not even get up. Bed felt like the safest place; even though I was tormented by voices, at least I wasn't in a car when these things told me I should just end myself.

I was never taught anything about demons in church. I learned nothing about spiritual warfare. The church we went to taught that miracles ended in the Book of Acts, and Christians can't have demons, so I should just keep crucifying the flesh. There was no help for my child.

It came to a boiling point when I was alone in a hotel room with a Glock 17 and a single 9 mm bullet. In my despair I said one more prayer: "Father, show me who the real enemy is. Show me how to fight, because I can't."

I opened up my Facebook, and the first thing I saw was an ad for John Ramirez's Spiritual Warfare Bootcamp. I felt an urge like never before to take the class. I wept when I held the printed-out study guide and warfare prayers in my hands. Somehow I knew freedom was in those pages. I had very little faith, no training, nothing, but I knew this: anything was better than what it was.

The voices started silencing as I proclaimed the prayers. Somehow I had control over emotions that I never had control over before. I had no more thoughts of suicide. Oh and finally, I could hear the voice of the Holy Spirit.

As John taught us to break generational curses in the name of Jesus, speak life into hopeless situations, and declare the word of God, things changed for my daughter. Light started pouring in. She wanted to go to church with me; this was also not a church that did any spiritual warfare or deliverance, but it was at least a place where we could worship.

Finally, in December 2022, my daughter asked me if she could have deliverance too! By then I had taken all the classes and was part of the Inner Circle. After praying and yielding to the Holy Spirit, we went through renouncing and casting demons out, breaking off word curses, and repenting for her sins and sins of our ancestors. We prayed for forgiveness. Spirits manifested and left. The power of God was at work in our home, delivering my girl and setting her free. We prayed for the Holy Spirit to fill her.

The next day she asked to be baptized in the river. After her baptism, she threw away her vapes and weed. She went from dark to light, from walking around in an atmosphere of hell to walking around in the kingdom realm of heaven.

She's a beautiful young woman. Eight months later she got married to a wonderful, godly young man, and she's currently carrying my first granddaughter, Eliana (meaning "my God has answered") Rose.

Her generation suffers the most under demonic oppression that I can tell. The enemy is using any means—Disney, Hollywood, social media, and school—to steal our children's identity. And the church for the most part is asleep.

But God is raising up a remnant, an army of mothers and fathers who are not afraid and are trained and equipped by the Holy Spirit and people like John Ramirez. The love for our children and spouses will always move heaven on their behalf. The blood of Jesus still saves. The stripes of Jesus still heal. And demons must leave at the mention of His name.

I think God has a prayer box. It's colorful with colors in heaven called the testimonies of all time. Every time He pulls out a prayer, ready to color a beautiful thing in your life, He overrides the gloom and doom and darkness in your life. He puts in His special color and gives it life, brightening up that area of your life that was once dead. You become the coloring book. This is how I think about the beautiful testimonies of heaven in our lives. It is one way of describing God's infinite love for us. Thank You, Jesus.

TESTIMONY OF IMANUEL

I connected with the Inner Circle in early September 2023 with the harkening of the Holy Spirit while being broken and hurt in my heart and spirit. I was told to connect with John Ramirez as I was in the process of deliverance from freemasonic witchcraft, satanic programing, and witchcraft manipulation. I was breaking free from the strongholds of the doctrine of men in the church. While I was connected to the Inner Circle group and in the refiner's fire, Abba used John Ramirez through the mentoring of the Holy Spirit to help me. I needed to break down the demonic holds in my life that were trying to block the blessings in my life; to dismantle the devil's evil influences from a witch; and to admit to using tarot cards, using crying spells to dictate my future and movements, illegally operating, and trying to come against financial blessings. Abba moved me forward and lifted me high on eagle's wings above the snake line, and He prepared my hands and feet for battle so I can be a testimony to others for the winning of souls.

Wow! Amazing, powerful miracles from heaven once again.

TESTIMONY OF ERICA ACOSTA

My name is Erica Acosta. I am now 26 years old. I became "ill" in 2019, but I became very ill in 2022–2023. I was on the edge of my deathbed for a whole year. Those were some very dark, painful years lost, and I felt like a shell in a body. I didn't know what happened to me, how and why I was in a body that didn't feel like my own. I was just consumed with toxic relationships or trying to have one.

My life before that was, well, complicated. I never cared about myself. I never loved myself. I was an unfit mother, but I was still a mother. I started to go out with some boy from my school. It started as just being friends but turned into way more than I even thought in my head. I started using drugs with this boy. We started dating and being together all the time. I was just running around, meeting toxic people, being in very uncomfortable places, and staying away from my parents and my sons at home. I would just be with this boy who I thought loved me. Years of drug use and only seeing my children off and on went by. I ended up in jail for something very stupid. I would do anything my boyfriend would tell me. I was very gullible, and he knew it.

I spent two years in jail, then went to a court-ordered rehab. I then began thinking and having a clear mind, which made things a lot worse. My court order was set for when I got out. It was a permanent court hearing to decide whether I would get my boys back.

I had very high hopes of getting them back. I prayed to God, Jesus Christ, the whole time [I] was in jail, begging Him for help and telling Him I'd change, so I thought for sure I was going to leave that day and get them. Things took a very big turn. I lost all my rights.

I left with a hole in my heart. I was unspeakably depressed, more than I've ever been my whole life. I became very numb. I remember all I wanted was my kids.

I met this other man and ended up moving in with him. Within literally a few days, this man acted weird. At first I felt as if it were kind of the same man somehow. I don't know, but they acted a lot alike. They were both very obsessive. This man kept me at his house away from my parents. He would hate it if I went to see them or started a huge argument if I told him I was going to see them. I started going every Sunday for church with them. I found out I was pregnant by him on Thanksgiving. I didn't want to be.

At the time I didn't want another child because I didn't have my own, but God wanted me to for some reason. I ended up having a son with that man.

When I first was with my boyfriend, his mother was the sweetest mother I ever met, letting me stay at her house with her son without paying rent. He was thirty-three years old with no job and still lived with his mother. He started our relationship off with lies, saying he lived by himself. Even when I found out the truth, I still went.

One day I was arguing with him. He was tired of going to Abilene, where my parents were. He was really fed up with my parents getting my head clearer about our relationship, which they did every time. He would keep me away from them as much as he could, telling me I needed to grow up already, telling me I didn't need to see my parents all the time. I told him no matter what, I'll always be close to my family. He then got very upset and looked at the TV screen, and I saw something I've never seen before in my entire life. His forehead changed, and his eyebrows went together. His eyes became a different color, and a film went over his eyes, something like a snake, reptilian.

I started getting very sick when I continued living there. I would eat his mother's food every once in a while, and I would get so sick, like I had the flu. I felt paralyzed, depressed, and barely able to take care of my son. I called my parents to come pick me up, which made my boyfriend and his mother all upset. His mother even came to talk to me about staying, but I had my mind made up. God had shown me too many things.

I began to start feeling weak in 2020, and it wasn't gradual. I was running out of breath when I never used to, I was forgetting a lot, my legs hurt all the time, and my head started to bother me. I began losing weight. My attitude changed. I fell back into depression more than ever. I didn't know what was going on. Every time I would eat, I would feel nauseous. I couldn't eat meat, as it would disgust me. My teeth started hurting and breaking into pieces, which made me very depressed. My front teeth were gone. I hurt everywhere, from my mouth to the rest of my body, every night.

Before all this, I weighed 130 pounds. I had a beautiful smile and was always happy, and I never questioned God. After this, I blamed Him, but it was my own choices that allowed the world to hit me. I opened my bubble of protection, and let evil in. I didn't know how to shut it. I knew all the problems I had at such a young age were not normal.

I was demonically attacked, and I had no clue. No matter what I ate, I wouldn't gain any weight. I would lose weight out of nowhere. I hated myself because it was all my own fault for letting my guard down, for not believing my parents. I fought demons mentally every single day, thinking I was fighting my own conscience, but it was really the spells and evil.

God was still with me and always had been. I ignored Him, but He never left me. I left Him. I ended up very ill, very ignorant. My family started praying for me and over me, but nothing changed. I gave God back my all, but I felt very ashamed that I gave it to Him only when I needed Him.

My parents found a doctor, and I started seeing him in 2022. By then I only weighed 80 pounds. I was in and out of the hospital for days. The infections in my body started getting worse out of nowhere. Tests were run almost every single day by many different specialists in town, but they did not know what was wrong with me. I was in and out of ICU three times with very bad infections in my lungs. The doctors found nothing that was causing it. The second time I had sepsis. They didn't know why I was having so much pain everywhere, why my teeth were coming out, or why I was losing weight every day and never gaining. I ended up in a walker.

Around March, my blood pressure would run 60/50 every day. My doctors were confused and called it a mystery sickness. They said they had never seen a patient like me. I then realized it was not a sickness from something; it was a spell, a very bad one.

My parents had tried to warn me, but I didn't know what to do about it. I would dig into the Bible but continued to get weaker and sicker. I kept reading, and the more I did, the worse I would get physically and emotionally. I would cry every night, quietly begging God for help, begging Jesus Christ to please take my pain, to please let the doctors find something. It was becoming hard to wake up in the morning, both physically and emotionally. My blood pressure would drop so low I would almost be in a coma every night. In the morning, I would get up drained and exhausted, with my legs going numb, making it hard to walk. My teeth were still falling out, and my bones were getting frailer. I just kept reading the Bible, awaiting my death at the age of twenty-six. I began to say my goodbyes.

On June 24, 2023, my parents were so excited because they heard this man was coming down from New York. His name was Evangelist John Ramirez. He is a very strong man and has had a lot of evil happen in his life now that he changed his life to help others with spells and all this other stuff through the Holy Spirit. I was excited, thinking it was my last chance.

When I arrived, I was very scared. I was using my walker. I was barely walking. I was sitting on it, and my mom was pushing me because I had no strength to even stand at times. I was always light-headed. Then the service started, and they called everyone to talk or pray. I can hardly remember the first day, but I do remember being down there with my walker. It felt as if Evangelist Ramirez just ran up to me and forced his hand on my head, and then I blacked out. I don't remember. I just remember him asking me to come again the next day. I barely slept. I pushed myself back the next day. I barely wanted to go. I don't know why I was excited, but my spirit wasn't going the next day.

I went down again, and there he was. I remember my heart pounding as he came up to me. I never felt so scared inside. He put his hand on my head and said that he saw a cult. He asked what cult I was in. I said none. I didn't know what he was talking about. With my parents holding me on each side, he asked again what cult I was in. I stated, "I don't know. I never have been in one of those evil things."

My mother then asked if it could be one of my soul ties to the occult, and Evangelist Ramirez said yes. He started praying over me. I can't remember what. I yelled, "No, no," two or three times and then cried aloud with everything in me. I busted out yelling, "Yes yes," to what he was saying. I gave it all to God, to Jesus Christ.

I then passed out. After waking, I got up and realized I was standing on my own. I ran to my parents saying, "It worked. I'm better. Jesus Christ has healed me through this amazing, powerful man." I remember seeing Evangelist Ramirez with a shocked, confused look on stage. When it was over, I ran up to him and gave him a huge hug. Ever since then I've been so thankful and grateful that Evangelist Ramirez came down and delivered me from the occult.

Because of Evangelist Ramirez, I was saved by Jesus Christ. I get to wake up happy every day. My church is the Rise Church in Abilene, Texas, with Pastor Ray. So many people have seen deliverance there.

I won't go back to looking for a father for my children. There is so much evil in this world. All it takes is one opening or one invitation, and evil has you for life if you don't know how to fight back spiritually. I found out that all I needed was God, Jesus Christ, the true Father, Son, and Holy Spirit. That's the best Father my children could ever have, and the One who will always be there with us.

P.S. I am now traveling and taking vacations with my kids and family. I am able to drive. I haven't been admitted into a hospital since that summer. I haven't had infections. I'm better and staying that way. I'm a new me mentally, spiritually, and physically. Thank You, Jesus.

Only God can write this masterpiece of a beautiful testimony. What the devil meant for evil, God turned around for good. Praise be to God in Jesus' mighty name. Amen.

Testimony of Josephine

In 2021 my husband, Jason, and I traveled to a conference John was speaking at so he could pray with us. We had been married for three years and had had seven miscarriages. We both had deep desires for children, but we didn't understand why there continued to be roadblocks and heartbreak. The Holy Spirit moved Jason and me to attend a live conference to meet John in person and ask him to pray for us. We were not disappointed. John is one of the most down-to-earth men of God you could ever meet. He immediately made us feel comfortable, and he prayed a powerful prayer for us, stating the Lord would bless us with a boy and a girl.

A year later I got pregnant with a baby girl, but we lost her at twenty weeks. Eivissa went to heaven early to be with the Lord, and we were utterly devastated. Jason and I felt we must have done something to cause this and felt we perhaps didn't deserve children. John Ramirez continued to minister to us and pray with us, saying, "Job went through intense trials, but it didn't mean he was not favored by God." He again encouraged us that God would bless us with a boy and girl. At that point, we would have been happy with just one child.

Jason and I continued to pray faithfully even during the darkest times of our life following the death of our baby girl. In February of 2023 I got pregnant again, but we did not tell anyone, praying each day for the Lord to provide. We are excited to share in November 2023, God blessed us with a boy and a girl, Micah and Ellyse.

Thank you, Dr. John Ramirez, for being a humble servant of the Lord and for dedicating your life to helping His people. Thank you, Holly Brunson, for your prayers and servant heart.

> Like arrows in the hands of a warrior are children born in one's youth. Blessed is the man whose quiver is full of them. They will not be put to shame when they contend with their opponents in court.
> —PSALM 127:4–5

God is an awesome God. He works miracles, signs, and wonders every day. Don't miss your miracle. The miracle is never delayed. The miracle will never be forgotten. God is working it out for you today.

This is the Word of the Lord: "And they overcame him by the blood of the Lamb and by the word of their testimony, and they did not love their lives to the death" (Rev. 12:11, NKJV).

Chapter 9

TEN THOUSAND THOUGHTS

IT HAS BEEN estimated that ten thousand thoughts go through each of our minds on a daily basis. The Bible says, "For as he thinks in his heart, so is he" (Prov. 23:7, NKJV). In other words, you are what you think. So what are we going to do? Why does the enemy try so hard to turn you into something God never signed off on? Who will you believe? Ten thousand thoughts go through the door of your mind each day. Who are you willing to trust?

Your mind is a bad neighborhood. Don't walk through it by yourself. Bring the Holy Spirit with you. This is why we must have the mind of Christ (1 Cor. 2:16).

- **Right mind**—"Then they came to Jesus, and saw the one who had been demon-possessed and had the legion, sitting and clothed and in his right mind. And they were afraid" (Mark 5:15, NKJV).

- **Sober mind**—"...but hospitable, a lover of what is good, sober-minded, just, holy, self-controlled" (Titus 1:8, NKJV).

- **Sound mind**—"For God has not given us a spirit of fear, but of power and of love and of a sound mind" (2 Tim. 1:7, NKJV).

- **Spiritual mind**—"For to be carnally minded is death, but to be spiritually minded is life and peace" (Rom. 8:6, NKJV).

If you walk alone in your mind without the Holy Spirit, the devil will have leverage over you. His goal is to redirect and derail your mind with these conditions:

- **Anxious mind**—"And do not seek what you should eat or what you should drink, nor have an anxious mind" (Luke 12:29, NKJV).

- **Debased mind**—"And even as they did not like to retain God in their knowledge, God gave them over to a debased mind, to do those things which are not fitting" (Rom. 1:28, NKJV).

- **Carnal mind**—"For to be carnally minded is death, but to be spiritually minded is life and peace" (Rom. 8:6, NKJV).

- **Worldly mind**—"Do not conform to the pattern of this world, but be transformed by the renewing of your mind. Then you will be able to test and approve what God's will is—his good, pleasing and perfect will" (Rom. 12:2).

The Bible also says we serve the Lord with our minds (Rom. 7:25).

My brothers and sisters in the Lord, I'm going to give it to you straight because I love you so much. We don't need predictions in our minds. Predictions are question marks. Predictions are of the world. Predictions are of the devil. We need truth in our minds and in our hearts. Truth will set us free. Predictions bring chaos, confusion, doubt, unbelief, and entrapment by the enemy. Truth is Christ all day, every day.

News flash: You can't believe everything that crosses your mind. Read what the apostle Paul says about our minds: "The weapons we use in our fight are not the world's weapons but God's powerful weapons, which we use to destroy strongholds. We destroy false arguments; we pull down every proud obstacle that is raised against the knowledge of God; we take every thought captive and make it obey Christ" (2 Cor. 10:4–5, GNT). This is spiritual warfare at its best. The fight is in the Scripture. The battlefield is in the Scripture.

You need to catch this teaching moment, this God moment for your mind, your life, your purpose, and your destiny. I think many of us are in the third quarter of the battle hoping for a win, a victory. If you want victory, you need to learn these lessons and expose the enemy on the one yard line of your life. You need to spiritually understand and comprehend the insights, the satanic strategies, the perversion, and the entrapment of the enemy and how he comes at you and for you. He dresses himself up as an angel of light. When we wait too long to open our spiritual eyes, we are already too deep in the fight and have lost a lot of spiritual ground in our minds.

Things happen in the physical world around you, but the battle starts in your mind. The enemy knows if he can incarcerate your mind and redirect it to his playground, then the rest of you will follow.

Surrender All to Have It All

I think we sometimes gloss over what the apostle Paul says in 2 Corinthians 10:4–5 when we read it. We learn nothing, we understand nothing, and we receive nothing from it spiritually. Our brother Paul is exposing the devil. He's shaming the devil. He's showing you where the devil is standing in your mind. I'm going to prove this to you so the next time he slips one demonic thought into your ten thousand, you will know how to destroy it, step all over it, and claim your victory.

Here's what Paul is telling us in 2 Corinthians 10:4–5: There are the bad neighbors in the neighborhood of your mind. Strongholds and false arguments live on the same street. Proud obstacles are other demonic neighbors trying to take over your thoughts and your words in order to hold your mind hostage.

But I have bad news for the devil. Jesus said in Matthew 22:37, "Love the Lord your God with all your heart, with all your soul, and with all your mind" (GNT). Do you see what the Lord Jesus Christ is telling us? Love the Lord your God with all your heart. Check mark. Love the Lord your God with all your soul. Check mark. Love the Lord your God with all your mind. Check mark. This is where the devil tries his best to come in the door to your ten thousand thoughts with his demonic forces. We need God to heal our minds so that we can love Him fully. Say this prayer with me right now:

> *Lord Jesus, I cancel every satanic assignment against me and every ungodly, unrighteous, demonic thought that has slipped through my ten thousand thoughts today into the living room of my mind. I destroy every false argument, every stronghold, and any proud*

thoughts right now with the blood of Jesus. Lord, heal my mind today. In Jesus' name, amen.

It's time to turn on the fire of the Holy Spirit in your mind. Let the furnace of your mind make the devil uncomfortable every time he tries to bring in diabolical thoughts, question marks, and deception.

STOP DRINKING THE SPIRITUAL KOOL-AID

The Bible says, "'Who has known the mind of the Lord so as to instruct him?' But we have the mind of Christ" (1 Cor. 2:16). That's how we should live. We must have the mind of Christ. There's no room for anything else.

If you're going through a challenge, don't let the devil convince you that you are less of a Christian. You're more than enough in the eyes of the Lord. Stay genuine and honor God.

If you take a one-hundred-dollar bill and throw it in the mud, step on it, and then pick it back up and take it to the grocery store to buy something with it, it still has the value of a one-hundred-dollar bill. Even though it's wrinkled, has some dirt on it, and might even smell funny, it's still a one-hundred-dollar bill. Just because you're going through a challenge, it doesn't mean you are not who God says you are.

The devil will fight you with everything he has, including the kitchen sink. Doubt, fear, anxiety, worry, and unbelief are the weapons he uses to incarcerate your mind, hoping to get one of his thoughts into your ten thousand. Stop asking, "Where is this coming from? Why is this happening? What's going on?" Those are distraction words straight from the devil's playbook. They keep you playing the game with him.

Here is the key. This is what I want you to catch in your spirit from head to toe: The devil wants to put feet to your thoughts so you act on them, play them out, and live them out. The enemy wants his thoughts to go from your head to your feet. That's the demonic game plan. That's why Christians backslide and walk away from the faith. That's why Christians commit suicide. It starts with a thought, and then they put feet to it—and that's right from the devil's playbook. Cut the feet off today and destroy the thoughts now, in Jesus' mighty name.

I want to share a testimony with you from my before-Christ life. When I was a ferocious warlock, one thing tormented me beyond human comprehension: the fear of flying and getting on planes. The fear was so horrific that I could stand at the window of an airport and stare at a plane and break into a cold sweat, with my heart beating ninety miles per hour. I had dream after dream that every plane I boarded fell into the ocean. I would wake up in a cold sweat.

I remember after my wife and I got married, we planned a honeymoon to Puerto Rico. I backed out at the last minute, and a girlfriend went with my wife on what was supposed to be our honeymoon. I was so tormented and rattled by just the thought of boarding a plane.

Soon after I got saved, the first opportunity the Lord gave me was to preach in a small church in Florida. I was excited about getting the opportunity to go somewhere I had never been, but in the back of my mind I heard the devil say, "If you get on the plane, you'll never make it to Florida. You will crash and burn."

The day came that I was supposed to fly out. I remember it was a snowy and dark day in New York City, and there was already snow on the ground. I headed to the airport, and the flight was delayed. I left the airport and booked a Greyhound bus with a very dear friend of mine. We took the bus all the way down the East Coast to Florida. We got there. We accomplished the mission by preaching the gospel. Many were saved, healed, and delivered, even though I was just a young minister.

When the time came to travel home, I ran to Amtrak and jumped on a train headed back to New York. It was torture. It took hours. It was a day later when I arrived in New York City. There I was, proud and feeling good about myself, thinking, "Yes. I preached the gospel. I went to Florida. God is happy. I made it happen. I'm good. Everything is good. Jesus Christ is proud of me."

A moment later I heard the Holy Spirit say to me, "God is grieved with you. All this trip to Florida and everything that God used you for is not recorded in heaven. You get no credit for that because you never took the plane and did what God told you to do."

My heart broke. After all that took place, I let Jesus Christ down because of my doubt, fear, and unbelief. Ten thousand thoughts, and three got in. The devil put feet to those thoughts, and I walked the wrong way. I felt shame, guilt, and despair.

But God is the God of second chances. Is He giving you one today? If He can do it for me, He can do it for you.

God gave me the same exact opportunity to go somewhere else in Florida. This time I got on the plane. Once I was in my seat, I grabbed the white bag in front of me in case I needed to throw up. I was nervous and shaking like a leaf. My nervousness was so obvious that the lady sitting next to me asked, "This is the first time you're flying?"

I asked, "How do you know?"

She said, "Umm, I can tell. I'm here. If you need anything to help you, to encourage you, please let me know."

God had placed someone right next door to me to bring

comfort to my anxiety, my doubt, and my fears. That day I was set free. Never again was I tormented to get on any plane.

Today, because of the Lord Jesus Christ, I fly on planes 80 or 90 percent of the time to do what Jesus has called me to do, to live out my purpose and my destiny, and to crush the head of the serpent on the other side. How great is our God!

STOP MAKING PERMANENT DECISIONS DURING TEMPORARY BATTLES; WAIT ON THE LORD

We read in the Old Testament about a man named David. He was one of the greatest men in the Bible. How awesome David was. God even called him "a man after my own heart" (Acts 13:22). What a testimony!

David's story shows us how the devil can slip one thought in among our ten thousand. David was only a few chapters away from becoming king. How challenging life gets when you are so close to your new season, the next chapter of your purpose and your destiny. That's when the devil viciously tries to make sure that of the ten thousand thoughts you think each day, one of his makes it into your mind. That's what happened to David.

First Samuel 27:1 says, "Then David said to himself, 'Now I will perish one day by the hand of Saul. There is nothing better for me than to safely escape into the land of the Philistines. Then Saul will despair of searching for me anymore in all the territory of Israel, and I will escape from his hand'" (NASB).

My brothers and sisters, listen to me carefully. This is where the devil accomplished his mission. He put feet to David's thoughts by getting David to tell himself he would "perish one day by the hand of Saul." There you go. That's how fear got in. This is why you have to be very careful about what you think, what crosses your mind. Unfortunately, David allowed the enemy to bypass the door of his mind by telling himself he would perish.

That is the open door: "Now I will perish." David declared death upon himself. He stopped trusting God at that very moment, after he had seen so many miracles and God had saved his life from the hands of King Saul.

First Samuel 27:2 says, "So David set out and went over, he and the six hundred men who were with him, to Achish the son of Maoch, king of Gath" (NASB). I want you to understand this: When you allow the devil to put feet to your thoughts, not only do you have to face the consequences, but there is also a domino effect that brings your whole family with you. Whatever the thought is, it doesn't only affect you; it also affects others. This is what the devil wants to do all day, every day. As soon as David arose and crossed over, it was mission accomplished. The devil got what he wanted.

Let me say this—and I say it with a lot of love: you're only as sick as your mind and your thoughts. David's thoughts caused him to run in the wrong direction, and he lived in the land of the Philistines for one year and four months, out of God's perfect will.

If you find yourself in that place today, whatever your circumstances are or your situation is, there is good news for you in this chapter. You can be set free and get back to God's perfect will for your life. When you put feet to the devil's thoughts, he will entrap you, which is his game plan. This is what the devil calls checkmate in the chess game between him and the Lord Jesus Christ. How could David go to the land of Gath when years earlier he'd killed their best man, Goliath? God is good. He's here for you today.

So where do we go from here? Read 1 Samuel 30:6: "David was

greatly distressed because the men were talking of stoning him; each one was bitter in spirit because of his sons and daughters. But David found strength in the LORD his God." There you go, my brothers and sisters. David found strength in the Lord his God. That's where the victory is, not at the demise of the enemy. When the devil got his thoughts into David's mind and then put feet to them, David found strength in the Lord his God.

That is the secret weapon you need today. Find strength in the Lord your God. It's not where you start that's important; it's where you finish. This is a spiritual warfare moment. The Scriptures tell us that David fought his way back and crushed the head of the devil. And David wasn't the only one who came back; the six hundred men came back as well. When God restores, He does a complete job.

It's time to pray and cut the toes and feet off your thoughts. This is spiritual warfare at its best, in Jesus' mighty name. Pray these prayers with me:

> *Devil, I put you on notice. Today you will be evicted from my mind because I have the mind of Christ, in Jesus' name.*
>
> *I release the voices in my head. Let them drown; let them be destroyed in the blood of Jesus.*
>
> *I release the voice of the Holy Spirit and the blood of Jesus to destroy all manipulations against me in my thoughts, my thinking, and my heart today, in Jesus' incredible, awesome name. Amen.*
>
> *I soak my life and my thoughts in the blood of Jesus.*

I paralyze all satanic oppressions and depressions that are trying to penetrate my mind, my thinking, and my reasoning and block out the voice of the Holy Spirit. I drown those devils in the blood of Jesus.

I hold the blood of Jesus as a shield over my mind to protect me from any powers of darkness that are trying to poison my mindset. In the name of Jesus Christ, amen.

I stand upon the spoken Word of God and declare myself unshakable and unmovable in this season and in the one to come, in the awesome, all-powerful name of my Lord and Savior, Jesus Christ.

Chapter 10

GOD MOMENTS

I WANT TO SHARE four incredible God moments with you. You can fit yourself into these stories and make them your own.

GOD MOMENT: HOLLYWOOD IN NYC

I heard an amazing story that took place in New York City. There was a gathering, and the main speaker of the event was a very famous Hollywood actor with an iconic voice. If I were to tell you this actor's name, you would know him because of his unique, distinguished voice.

The atmosphere at the event was electrifying. The house was packed with people who admired this actor's movies, his documentaries, and his voice. Everyone was excited to see this man front and center, answering questions as people raised their hands. It sounded like a symphony in Carnegie Hall throughout the night as he quoted lines from movies and documentaries that he took pride in being a part of with his beautiful voice.

It just so happened that there was a pastor in the audience that night. The pastor raised his hand, and the actor picked him out of the massive crowd, asking him, "Which part of a movie or documentary would you like me to say?"

The pastor smiled politely and humbly. He said, "I just wanted to see if you could quote Psalm 23 for us today."

The actor smiled, gestured with his hand, nodded his head, and said, "Absolutely, I could do that for you, but on one condition: After I'm done, it will be your turn."

The pastor looked at the actor and smiled, and in a voice that was broken from years of preaching he agreed that he would do it right after the actor. The actor started quoting Psalm 23 (NKJV), his melodious voice ringing through the halls of the event:

> The LORD is my shepherd; I shall not want. He makes me to lie down in green pastures; He leads me beside the still waters. He restores my soul; He leads me in the paths of righteousness for His name's sake. Yea, though I walk through the valley of the shadow of death, I will fear no evil; for You are with me; Your rod and Your staff, they comfort me. You prepare a table before me in the presence of my enemies; You anoint my head with oil; my cup runs over. Surely goodness and mercy shall follow me all the days of my life; and I will dwell in the house of the LORD forever.

It was an amazing moment. Everyone stood up. The actor received a five-minute standing ovation of people clapping, whistling, screaming, and yelling out "Bravo!"

Now it was the pastor's turn. He got up from his seat and started to quote, "The LORD is my shepherd..." When he got to the end of the psalm, there was no standing ovation. There was no clapping. There was no "Bravo." There was no whistling. But no one in the room could hold back their tears. Every person in that place was teary-eyed, to the amazement of the reporters who were at the event.

The reporters ran over to the actor, asking him, "What happened? What happened? What happened?"

The actor bowed his head and said, "I knew the words, but he knew the God of the Word."

And that should be the story of every believer. It's not good enough to know the Word; we need to know the God of the Word. That should be our biggest desire as we walk the Christian journey—to know the God of the Word. Let that be your story.

GOD MOMENT: YOU CAN FIND CHRIST'S MESSAGE IN A MASTERPIECE

There is a famous painting by the painter George Frederic Watts. People say that a picture is worth a thousand words. I think this painting says it all.

It's a painting of a woman sitting on a rock. You can't tell if she is in a desert or in a storm—the artist sort of blurred that part out and kept it hidden away—but it's clear she is in a dire situation. She is sitting there on a rock, blindfolded, and playing the harp. The amazing thing about the harp is all the strings are gone except one. The name of this beautiful painting is *Hope*.[1]

That just says it all. Even if you can't see and you only have one string left, I'm telling you there is hope for your situation if you're sitting on the Rock, Jesus Christ. Listen, my brothers and sisters. It doesn't matter if you're in the desert or in a storm, like the young lady in the painting; you're in God's perfect will when you sit on Jesus Christ the Rock. Even though you can't see what's in front of you, your next step, or what's ahead, I'm telling you there is always hope—just like the name of the painting—for the people of God.

In the midst of any report, God won't let you down. I promise you that. There's hope for today, there's hope for tomorrow, and there's hope always. Even though your heart might have only one string left, like the woman's harp in the painting, there is victory. All you need is one.

The painting reminds me of Paul and Silas in the Book of Acts, when they were beaten and thrown in the inner part of the jail for setting a young lady free from a demon through the power of the Holy Spirit. All they had in the prison was one string and their worship. Suddenly an earthquake shook the foundation of the jail, the prison cells were opened, and their chains fell off (Acts 16:16–26).

Let that be your story, in Jesus' mighty name.

God Moment: Be Known as a Man or Woman of Prayer

Here is another amazing story a pastor friend once told me about a well-known preacher who had a school and an orphanage in London in the 1800s. During that time, God told him to search for a building in downtown London because He wanted him to put a building there for the children.

This preacher got up and started a journey to look for the building God had spoken to him about. As he went through downtown London, looking and searching, he saw a building from a distance that was for sale. He walked into that building, and the real estate representative for the owners of the building happened to be there that day. The preacher went in, looked around, and asked the realtor what the price of the building was.

The realtor gave him a ridiculous number—let's just say $500,000.

The preacher told the realtor, "I'll make an offer of $50,000."

The realtor said, "This is ridiculous and absurd. What kind of offer is this?"

The preacher just looked at him politely, smiled, and said, "Here's my business card. If you change your mind, give me a call, and I want to move forward to purchase the building." Then he left.

The evening of that same day, the owners of the building stopped by to see the realtor. The owner asked, "Did we get any offers on the property?"

The real estate man said, "Only one man came in here. He made a ridiculous offer. I mean, I'm so embarrassed to even tell you about it. He left his business card here."

The building owner looked at the business card and recognized the name. "*This* is the man who made the offer?"

The realtor said, "Yup. That's the guy. He made a $50,000 offer for your building." The realtor shook his head and said, "What a ridiculous offer. I'm ashamed to even share this information with you."

The owner of the building looked at the business card intensely. He asked, "This man was here at my building to look at it, and he made an offer?"

The realtor said, "Yup, that's the man. He came here and made the ridiculous, terrible offer for your building."

The owner took a deep breath and said to the realtor, "Go get the money now, because if that man starts to pray, he will get the building for free."

What an amazing story about how people can recognize the power of prayer. Many of us underestimate the power of prayer. The businessman quivered and shook because he knew that preacher knew how to pray and touch heaven. Let that be your story, wherever your journey and your walk with the Lord takes you—that people will know that if you pray, heaven will move on your behalf; that lives will change because you know how to pray and touch heaven on your behalf and theirs. God is good.

GOD MOMENT: SPIRITUAL BOOT CAMP AT ITS BEST (NO COP-OUTS OR EXCUSES)

Michael Phelps is an amazing swimmer. He reached the Olympics and won a record twenty-eight medals. I heard a story about his early years in the swimming pool, when he trained at North Baltimore Aquatic Club and he and his coach had an amazing dream together. In the story the coach is a symbol of God, and Michael Phelps is a symbol of us as we walk with God.

During his training, Michael would jump into the pool, and the coach would have him swim laps back and forth, hundreds and hundreds and hundreds of times. He was training Michael to be an Olympic gold medal winner. The coach was known for doing the unpredictable during training. There was even a time he turned off the lights and had Michael swim in the dark, back and forth. He was training him to understand and to know the journey in the pool from one side to the other.

Another time, the coach stepped on Michael's goggles, damaging them right before a race. When Michael hit the water, his goggles flooded with water, and he couldn't see the end of the pool. But because he had swum so many times with different kinds of challenges, from darkness to broken goggles, he knew how to reach the other side. He mastered swimming in all kinds of unpredictable conditions.[2]

Michael Phelps stood on the starting block in Beijing, China, during the Olympics, put on his goggles, and dove into the pool. He started to swim, and out of nowhere his goggles started to fill up with water, so much so that he couldn't see anything—but he kept swimming. He remembered the training that his coach gave him when he was swimming in the dark or with leaking goggles.

Michael Phelps kept swimming back and forth, blind and with goggles full of water. He knew the pool in his mind; he knew how many strokes it took to get from one end to the other. When he reached the end of the pool when the race was over, he heard the yells and screams and cheers of the crowd.[3] When Michael took off his goggles and looked up at the board, he saw that not only had he won the gold medal, but he had broken the world record in the 200-meter butterfly. What an amazing story.

I think God, in His awesome ways, trains us in the dark. He allows things to happen, and we can't see what's in front of us. But we keep swimming from one side to the other because we trust Him and love Him. We know He has our backs because He was faithful to train and prepare us for unpredictable moments on our unpredictable journeys, even in the dark. Sometimes our vision gets blurry and we can't see the next step, but that's when we remember the training in faith that God has given us, and we know we will reach the finish line even though we don't see what's in front of us. Every stroke we take is a stroke of faith, knowing that the Master is leading the way.

Let that be your story in your walk with the Lord Jesus Christ and the Holy Spirit as the ultimate coach. To God be the glory, honor, and praise and all the worship in this journey called Christianity.

Who Holds the Pen of Your Story?

How amazing are these stories! At the end of every story is a beacon of light, a torch. The first story lets us know that it's not just about knowing the Word but knowing the God of the Word. In the second story, the painting tells it all. It doesn't matter if you're in the desert or in the storm, if you're blindfolded, or if you have a harp that has only one string. When you're sitting on the Rock that is Jesus Christ, the hope of glory, you will see tomorrow—you're sitting on the victory.

The third story is a powerful one. Let people know that you're a man or woman of prayer. When you pray, heaven stops and moves on your behalf. The fourth story teaches us that no matter how dark, unpredictable, or uncertain times get, with the Lord Jesus Christ by our side and the power of the Holy Spirit we can swim in the dark in any pool, at any given time, in any circumstances, situation, or season. God made us. He created us to swim in the dark, to trust Him because He is the ultimate Coach of all time. Amen.

Chapter 11

THE WOKE CHURCH

THE WORLD HAS sent a plain and clear message to the church at large today. When I say the world, I mean the systems of the world that belong to the devil. That is spiritual warfare on a different scale. We have left it untouched, and now we have created a monster. That monster is telling the church, "Be silent and step down. Now we have become the woke church."

This "woke" church has come into agreement with the devil and his demonic systems of the world. Because the world has taken God out of the equation, this is what they do now. When they can't fix something, they legalize it and make it the norm. But just because something is legal here on the earth doesn't mean it's legal in heaven.

We are living in a place where no one is talking about this kind of spiritual warfare. We have no problem talking about demons in the church. We easily talk about Jezebel, marine spirits, python spirits, and husband spirits, and we identify with those demons and that platform. But there is one spirit that has the world running toward the edge of the cliff.

I have made the choice to be brave enough and tough enough to run in the opposite direction and expose what needs to be exposed. Call me crazy. Call me mad. I can live with that because

I've learned in my walk with the Lord that I don't live based on the opinions of people; I live by the truth of God.

Someone needs to address the elephant in the room. But there are two animals in this room: an elephant and an ostrich. The elephant in the room is the demonic systems of the world. The ostrich in the room is the woke church with its head in the sand, hoping the elephant will leave the room—but no one is pushing him out.

We have allowed these demonic false identities and principalities to run our nation, our country, and our world. What blows my mind is how we are so in love with religion. We have allowed the Vatican and the Pope and demonic systems in Catholicism to run the show and open Christianity to demons.

In this day and age when truth is called insanity, who is going to address the elephant in the room? When you address the demonic, it's called spiritual warfare. Who did it better than Jesus when He addressed the leaders of His day, the demonic of His day, the contradictions of His day, and the conflicts of His day? Jesus confronted them head-on with love *and* with truth.

Think about this powerful quote: "When the whole world is running towards a cliff, he who is running in the opposite direction appears to have lost his mind." That would be me, and I'm OK with that because the world is running toward the edge of the cliff, and someone has to save them.

I say this with a heavy heart. I remember 9/11 in New York City. From the rooftop of the building that I lived in I could see the smoke from the burning towers. How many thousands of people ran out of those buildings like they had never run before in their whole lives? I praise God for the many who made it out. But here's the thing: while many wonderful people were running out of the buildings to save their lives, firefighters were running in, knowing they would lose their lives. I have always been perplexed by that because when danger shows up, our human instinct is to run the other way, not toward the danger.

I guess that will be my story in this chapter. I'm going to run in the opposite direction, away from the cliff. I'm going to sound the alarm and sound the trumpets by exposing the demonic systems of the world that have run unchecked for as long as I can remember.

I have been saved for twenty-four years. When I was in the devil's kingdom my job, my assignment, my mission was to astral project to curse the regions and reinforce them with demonic witchcraft. So I think I know a little bit about what's going on.

This Is No Time to Fall Asleep

The church has fallen asleep in the lap of Delilah, the lap of the world. As a result the enemy is running the show, using the news media, Hollywood, government, schools, sports, and social media. People are approaching the edge of the cliff and are perishing spiritually. The devil and his demonic kingdom are having their way, and time is running out.

We, the church, are the ostrich with its head in the sand. No one wants to confront spiritual warfare. Ephesians 6:12 says, "For our struggle is not against flesh and blood, but against the rulers, against the authorities, against the powers of this dark world and against the spiritual forces of evil in the heavenly realms." As believers, we don't attack people. We love people. They are made in the image of the Lord Jesus Christ. We do, however, attack and confront what's behind the scenes. I call it spiritual warfare of the highest levels for the woke church. I love Jesus Christ too much, as well as the church and the people of the world, to leave things the way they are.

In 1999 I was given the opportunity of a lifetime. Salvation came knocking at my door. I believe everyone in the world, regardless of who they are, what they've done, or what they're going through, deserves the same knock at the door. Revelation 3:20 says, "Here I am! I stand at the door and knock. If anyone hears my voice and opens the door, I will come in and eat with that person, and they with me."

It's time to wake up, get your head out of the sand, and be the church of Jesus Christ. People may think you lost your mind, but that's OK. You can tell them, "I lost my mind, and I'm in good company." Look at what the false prophet Shemaiah said in Jeremiah 29:26: "You are responsible to put into stocks and neck irons any crazy man who claims to be a prophet" (NLT). He called Jeremiah a "crazy man" because he told the truth. It blows my mind how the church—not the world, but the church—thinks a person is crazy just because he or she speaks the truth.

Jesus' family was no different. Mark 3:21 says, "When his family heard what was happening, they tried to take him away. 'He's out of his mind,' they said" (NLT). Think about that. Even our Lord Jesus Christ was called a madman for telling the truth.

The same thing happened to the apostle Paul when he preached the truth to the governor Festus. Scripture tells us, "Suddenly, Festus shouted, 'Paul, you are insane. Too much study has made you crazy!' But Paul replied, 'I am not insane, Most Excellent Festus. What I am saying is the sober truth'" (Acts 26:24–25, NLT).

The governor said, "What you preach is insane."

The apostle Paul said, "What I preach is the truth."

We all want to live in the neighborhood on the street called Politically Correct, but I will be the man running in the opposite direction, away from the cliff, sounding the trumpets and healing and confirming.

At the end of this chapter are some corporate prayers. I want all of you who are reading this book around the world to pray these prayers with me so we can confront the spiritual warfare that has gone on unchecked, unchallenged, and unconfronted for a very long time because the church refuses to get its head out of the sand, choosing instead to let the elephant sit in the room. We walk by the elephant. We walk around the elephant. Sometimes we even feed the elephant.

Not here. Not us. Not me.

"If it seems we are crazy, it is to bring glory to God. And if we are in our right minds, it is for your benefit" (2 Cor. 5:13, NLT). How do you like them apples?

Martin Luther changed Christianity in his time. He was not afraid to nail the Ninety-Five Theses (propositions for debate concerned with the question of indulgences) to the door of the church. He confronted and challenged the evildoers of his day and told them the truth. He was not afraid of engaging in spiritual warfare and bringing the truth right to the devil's face. In the words of this amazing man of God, "A preacher must be both soldier and shepherd. He must nourish, defend, and teach; he must have teeth in his mouth, and be able to bite and to fight."[1]

My teeth are ready, devil. My bite is hard through the power of the Holy Spirit.

God Never Called Me to Be an Ostrich

Today we are facing spiritual warfare at the highest level in the public square of our society. The church would rather be politically correct and act like the ostrich with its head in the sand than to step into the public square and engage in spiritual warfare to set the world free. I will call truth, truth; I will call lies, lies. I will be on the Lord's side until the day He calls me home.

We would rather face demons at events and conferences than in the public square. We deliverance ministers come to these events and love on our brothers and sisters, and by the power of the Holy Spirit and the gifts that God has given us, He sets captives free—and that's a good thing. I'm all into that. But there is a dying world out there that has been so infiltrated and incarcerated by the devil and his demonic systems that right is called wrong and wrong is called right. The church has not addressed this elephant that has been stinking up the room called the world.

These devils are trying to destroy the human race. Today we find ourselves with a society that is about to run off the cliff, and no one is saying anything. No one is sounding the trumpet. How cruel would it be for me to walk through your neighborhood at three in the morning, see a building on fire, stay quiet, and just keep walking home? Really? Did God save you for that? Did Jesus pay the ultimate price on the cross so you could walk by the burning building without sounding the alarm, knocking on the doors, and yelling from the bottom of your heart, "The building is on fire!" to those asleep in their apartments?

Call me mad. All the days of my life I will respect and honor the heroes—the firefighters, the paramedics, and others who run into burning buildings to save others. But I'm talking about this from the spiritual side. If you tell someone to turn around, they will probably think you're insane.

I say this with a broken heart: I have never received an invitation to speak from a megachurch—not that I'm asking for one. Please don't misunderstand. Think about it. The glory of God has left many megachurches. There is nothing wrong with a megachurch. You could say Peter had one when he preached the gospel after leaving the Upper Room and three thousand people got saved that day. But Peter preached the truth in the public square, risking his life and making Jesus Christ proud. And this was Peter—denying Peter; cursing Peter. He stepped out into the public square and told the world the truth. Their response was, "What must we do to be saved?" I'm cool with that. That will be me.

I heard the other day that two of my heroes of the faith, Nicky Cruz and Billy Graham, have brought more people to the Lord than anyone else. I would love to be the third person on that list.

The church has become mainstream, not holy ground. There are few TV shows, the real popular ones, the household names, that invite popular influential preachers to come on their shows. The devil knows who he can pick and put on a show. I think if they put me on one of those shows, they would cut it short and have security escort me out. That's because I come with the truth, not with my agenda. I come with the arsenals of heaven and the love of Jesus Christ because the people on these shows deserve to hear the knock on the door along with those who are tuning in.

As a believer, you are the church of Jesus Christ when you step out into the public square. Not everyone will go to a church, so we are the only Bible that many people will see. I call this the fifth gospel. As believers we all are the fifth gospel, out in the open in this demonic society. Many of us shine brightly in the church, but once we get out in the world we walk in doom and gloom.

The devil's weapons aim to legalize, change truth for lies, and promote false realities. If we hear something repeated enough times on the news and in social media, it sounds like the truth. But they are lies, false realities that keep people running toward the cliff. Let's confront the spiritual warfare elephant in the room.

The devil has his hand wrapped around the world. Someone needs to pry his fingers off once and for all. But the woke church doesn't want to step onto the battlefield. They would rather live on the love boat so as not to offend the devil and his demonic systems—but it's OK to offend Jesus at any given time. It's OK to let the enemy destroy our families, our children, our communities, and our human values that God created for us from the beginning of time. The church doesn't want to address present demonic issues. We just want nice talk.

Where is your courage? Where is your fight? It's time to kick the elephant out of the room. Where is your heart? Prayer wins. It's time for us to pray corporately, internationally, here and around the world. Raise up your voice, and together we will shake and rattle the devil's cage—the world. We've got this.

I remember hearing a story about a man who later became an amazing pastor at one of the largest churches in Canada today. He is on fire for the Lord and has been a special guest speaker at Times Square Church.

When this man was younger, he was deep into heavy metal rock and roll. One of the most influential heavy metal bands at the time was coming to his town as part of a worldwide tour. He purchased tickets, but his precious mother, who was sold out to Jesus, told her son, "You're not going to this concert."

He told his mama, "I'm going to this concert even if I have to go over your dead body."

She said, "I'm going to pray, and they aren't coming into our town."

Sure enough, prayer works. This precious woman of God sounded the alarm in Jesus Christ. The host of heaven heard her prayers, and the only event of the band's worldwide tour that was completely canceled was in her hometown. And that was just because one person prayed.

BAPTIZE ME, LORD, WITH FIRE

Let's get together and sound the battle cry. I love the story of Nehemiah, a man who was baptized in anguish. It is my plea for the woke church to get its head out of the sand and cry out and be baptized with anguish like Nehemiah was. He called on the people from everywhere to come together and build the walls in Jerusalem. I'm calling for people to come together to build the spiritual walls of America and the world.

At the end of Nehemiah's story we read about two devils, Sanballat and Tobiah, who showed up from time to time to intimidate Nehemiah and to bring hindrances, delays, blockages, doubt, and fear. But when God baptizes you with anguish and the anointing, those devils don't mean anything. You will keep building the wall with one hand and fighting the enemy with the other for the sake of the people.

I love the story of when David had four hundred men with him in a cave. They were armed and dangerous. I also love the story of Gideon. He had three hundred men in the battlefield, and they took out a vast army and gave God the victory.

How crazy does this sound today! Not too long ago the world was struck with COVID-19, and the church fell asleep for eighteen months. When we decided to wake up from this spiritual slumber, the devil had seized spiritual territory by changing the spiritual atmospheres of our schools and our homes, attacking our children, our families, our marriages, and our identities. Now, men want to be women. The devil wants to change our children's identities by making disgusting, filthy, despicable movies aimed at children. There is a push to put men who identify as women in women's sports to hurt our young ladies.

I don't have anything against a person who practices something that is unrighteous and unholy. My job is to pray for you. But when we talk about Christianity—when we tell people that Jesus loves them; when we ask them to come to church and say we want them to spend eternity in heaven—people get angry, upset, demonic, and diabolical on us, labeling us intolerant. Really? Read the words of Fulton J. Sheen: "Tolerance applies only to persons, but never to truth....Tolerance does not apply to truth or principles. About these things, we must be intolerant.... Right is right if nobody is right, and wrong is wrong if everybody is wrong. And in this day and age we need...'not a Church that is right when the world is right, but a Church that is right when the world is wrong.'"[2]

Listen to me. You can vote on policies, but you can't vote on truth. This is the madman talking, because the truth will set you free.

Read the words of Billy Graham, the amazing man of God: "You are never preaching until the audience hears Another Voice."[3] In other words, the audience is the world, and the other voice is the Holy Spirit—not my voice, but the voice of the Holy Spirit. The Bible says God is omnipresent, omniscient, and omnipotent. So when you don't obey what God says, you are saying you know better than God.

It's time for a spiritual reality check. We're letting the devil and the demonic systems of the world know that the church will arise and fight the good fight of faith for the people of the world.

The only way to fight a woke world is with an awakened church. I call out the liberal churches that are prophesying and have become the mouth of Satan to this dying world. Ephesians

5:13–14 (NLT) says, "But their evil intentions will be exposed when the light shines on them, for the light makes everything visible. This is why it is said, 'Awake, O sleeper, rise up from the dead, and Christ will give you light.'"

Peter ran down from the Upper Room to tell the truth. The apostle Paul ran to the public square to tell the truth. Stephen was stoned to death for telling the truth—but what an amazing moment it was: "But Stephen, full of the Holy Spirit, looked up to heaven and saw the glory of God, and Jesus standing at the right hand of God" (Acts 7:55). The Bible makes it clear that Jesus sits at the right hand of the Father, and our precious brother Stephen saw our Lord Jesus Christ standing. That had never happened in the Bible before. Jesus was standing for Stephen, and He stands for you and me today on the battlefield of spiritual warfare. Let's stop being influencers for social media and in our churches and start being soldiers for Christ.

When I was in the witchcraft world, I took a stand like never before. I put it all on the line during those twenty-five years. I put it all on the battlefield for the devil. I was not lukewarm. I was not spiritually soft. Now that I am in Christ, I'm not ashamed to take a stand for the kingdom of God for the sake of the world. I will not trade in my armor and dress like the woke church. I'm doing life in Jesus. I want no parole. I'm on death row.

Our nation is in a dangerous place. Second Corinthians 2:11 (NKJV) says, "...lest Satan should take advantage of us; for we are not ignorant of his devices." The devil's whispers echo in the world today, telling men they can be women, telling women they can be men, and telling our children they can make decisions on their own agenda because "It's your choice."

The devil is coming after our children. Where is the church? These children belong to God. The devil is a liar. There is a scripture that says, "But whoever causes one of these little ones who believe in Me to sin, it would be better for him if a millstone were hung around his neck, and he were drowned in the depth of the sea" (Matt. 18:6, NKJV).

It's time for the church to pray and confront the spiritual, corporate, satanic systems of the world. Instead of allowing them to bring down our spiritual walls, it's time we bring theirs down once and for all.

GOD'S LOVE FOR ALL

I want to address the LGBTQ+ by telling you the testimony of my brother Jimmy.

I remember as we were growing up, Jimmy played with Barbie dolls. He was not interested in playing with toys that were made for boys. I have news for you: he wasn't born that way. When you have curses and open demonic doors in your family, the devil will find where you are the weakest, the most vulnerable and defenseless, and create an opportunity to plague and torment you, and even to change your gender. We can fight the good fight of faith only when we're in Christ. Outside of Christ we are free lunch for the enemy.

When my brother grew up, he became a transvestite. He sang in transvestite clubs and dressed as a woman. He was bisexual and was married to a woman. My brother was also a witch doctor. He threw parties in his house to which no normal people were invited, only people who lived the life he lived. Some of them were addicted to alcohol and other substances. These parties in his home sometimes lasted for three days.

One day my brother had a heart attack because of his abuse of alcohol and cocaine. He was rushed to the hospital. I remember the Lord told me that day, "Go to the hospital and speak to your brother on My behalf."

I said, "I'm not going, Lord. He's going to have all those people there, and it's going to turn into a crazy fight, and I'm not looking forward to getting beat down."

The Lord said, "Obey Me and go."

I did. I went to the hospital and saw that my brother and his wife were the only ones in his room. When I stepped into the room, Jimmy yelled for me to leave. I told him, "Look. Before I leave, look out your window."

He did.

I said, "You could have been on that side of the street [at Calvary Hospital, a hospice facility], and God is giving you one opportunity to come to repentance."

The Holy Spirit took over that room and changed the atmosphere. His presence was so tangible at that moment. My brother and his wife wept, and they both received Jesus as their Lord and Savior that day.

My brother got baptized and filled with the Holy Spirit. He started going to church, and he went to discipleship class for one year. I remember he would tell me, "I'll make you a CD. I love this song," and it would be something like "How Great Is Our God" or "I Can Only Imagine." We would sit in the car and sing it together.

A week before my brother's birthday, he called my mom to tell her he would be there the next day at such and such a time to help her with the errands.

My brother closed his eyes a week before his birthday. But before he did, he told me, "I'm going to throw the most amazing Christian celebration in my home, and I'm going to invite all my friends."

I said, "Man, you better think twice about that because if those people manifest in your house and you're there by yourself, you better have 911 on standby," and we laughed.

That night he closed his eyes and went to meet Jesus. The Bible says tomorrow is not guaranteed to anyone. My brother did not have his birthday celebration. It never happened. But God had a greater plan.

At my brother's funeral, I preached the gospel. Jimmy was behind me in a box, but it was just the shell because he was in glory. I believe he was standing in the balcony of heaven that the Book of Hebrews speaks about, cheering me on: "You go, brother. You go, brother. Preach it. Preach it."

I preached John 3:16 (NKJV), "For God so loved the world that He gave His only begotten Son," because that's what the world needs to hear—not "You're going to hell" or "You're a sinner."

I remember that all the people, the misfits of society in the Bronx, came to the funeral that day to pay respects to my brother. Transvestites, homosexuals, bisexuals, drug dealers, and addicts came to the funeral. They all sat in the front. We didn't know who was who. We didn't know their stories. But Jesus does know each of their stories—He knows about their pain, their hurt, their letdowns, their betrayals, or who sexually abused them. God knows the whole story.

I preached the love of Jesus, and that evening eighteen of my brother's friends raised their hands and accepted Jesus as their Lord and Savior. My brother won eighteen souls that day. That was something to be celebrated on the earth and celebrated in heaven. While my brother was alive, he didn't win one soul to Jesus. But I stepped in his place and through the Holy Spirit won eighteen souls that evening. Heaven rejoiced, my brother rejoiced, and I rejoiced. We made Jesus Christ proud.

I'm going to address those who are LGBTQ+: I don't know what happened in your life, and I'm not making light of it, but I know the woke church is lying to you. They are liars and deceivers telling you that you can live that way—that you can be a man with a man or a woman with a woman, and that's love. But that's not the love that God designed for the human race.

The woke church is lying to the nations and staying in bed with the systems of the world that are run by the devil and his cronies. They say you can marry another man or marry another woman and be homosexual in the house of God. What an abomination. God loves the person but not the act.

I heard a story once about a man who decided to be adventurous and bring his girlfriend into the house of God to perform sexual acts. He died on the spot. It wasn't because God didn't love him. It was the act that was sinful—an abomination—and God couldn't tolerate it.

It's like the Christian who shacks up with his girlfriend. God loves the Christian people, but He hates the act of shacking up and not being joined in marriage. Sin is sin in the eyes of our Lord. Whether you shack up with your girlfriend or you practice unrighteous things with your body, it is still sin, and it hurts the heart of God because He has a better plan for you. He has a better purpose and destiny for you. If He were to show you, you would drop what you're doing and run to Him and embrace it. I promise you that. This is John Ramirez, a misfit for Jesus Christ, a nobody, a worthless person—but God knew my address when He found me in 1999.

You can boast about policy, but you can't change the truth. God is truth, and it cannot be changed, devil. I'm speaking for the kingdom. I'm speaking for our children. I'm speaking for our marriages. I'm speaking for our families. I'm speaking for the sake of the church.

Wake up to the reality of spiritual warfare. I'm not crazy; it's the truth. I'm not angry or hateful. I have a sense of urgency because the world is running toward the cliff and someone has to say something. The cry is for the nations, for the woke church, and for the LGBTQ+.

I have a question for you: What do you do when God's Word contradicts your lifestyle?

This is what the Word of the Lord says:

> Do you not know that the unrighteous will not inherit the kingdom of God? Do not be deceived. Neither fornicators, nor idolaters, nor adulterers, nor homosexuals, nor sodomites, nor thieves, nor covetous, nor drunkards, nor revilers, nor extortioners will inherit the kingdom of God. And such were some of you. But you were washed, but you were sanctified, but you were justified in the name of the Lord Jesus and by the Spirit of our God.
> —1 Corinthians 6:9–11, nkjv

This is for the wonderful people who are running in the wrong direction. Hear the Word of the Lord in Psalm 82 (nkjv):

> God stands in the congregation of the mighty; He judges among the gods. How long will you judge unjustly, and show partiality to the wicked? Selah
>
> Defend the poor and fatherless; do justice to the afflicted and needy. Deliver the poor and needy; free them from the hand of the wicked. They do not know, nor do they understand; they walk about in darkness; all the foundations of the earth are unstable. I said, "You are gods, and all of you are children of the Most High. But you shall die like men,

and fall like one of the princes." Arise, O God, judge the earth; for You shall inherit all nations.

Listen to the powerful words of R. C. Sproul, a precious man of God: "When God says something, the argument is over."[4] God wants the best for us.

To the woke church, listen to the Word of the Lord: "You let the world, which doesn't know the first thing about living, tell you how to live" (Eph. 2:2, MSG). You deny Jesus by doing so. You deny the Word of the Lord, and you deny the finished work of the cross. People are falling off the cliff because you want to be politically correct. You're afraid to kick the elephant out of the room and get your head out of the sand. But I will speak the truth. I will be the madman. I will be the crazy one, the one who will speak for the Lord Jesus Christ until the day He calls me home.

I Live Based on the Truth of God, not the Opinion of the World

If we are preaching and speaking the truth to the body of Christ, persecution will come. But I'm OK with that because I love Jesus Christ and I love every person that He made in His image.

I'm not a dreamer—far from it—but I once had a dream from God. In the dream I was arrested and put on an empty bus. I was being taken to a concentration camp for Christians. The thing that broke my heart was that the bus was empty. I was the only person on it. I was sitting on the right side of the bus, which the Lord showed me meant I was in right standing with the Lord. The bus represented ministry, a convoy to bring the gospel. I remember passing by a building and seeing to my left an army of men in army fatigues rushing out of the building to go get more people. Throughout the dream I had peace and joy knowing I had fought the good fight for Jesus Christ and for the people God loves who live in the world that He made.

To the nations and to the world I say, "Stay right where you are. We're coming for you." I put the devil on notice that the people of God are coming with powerful, corporate prayers that will bring down the darkness covering the nations. We will put the banner of the cross of Jesus Christ back where it belongs.

I will be like the little girl by the sea who saw hundreds of starfish on the sand and ran to as many as she could, putting them back into the water.

One person asked the girl, "Hey, what are you doing? You're not going to make a difference."

She said, "Maybe not to you, but it will make all the difference to each starfish."

When we speak the truth, people may say, "What are you doing? You're not going to make a difference."

We can respond, "Maybe not to you, but it will mean everything to Jesus Christ because He loves the world He made and the people in it."

I can prove it to you: "For God so loved the world that He gave His only begotten Son, that whoever believes in Him should not perish but have everlasting life" (John 3:16, NKJV). That's the signature of heaven. You only need to say, "Lord Jesus, forgive me for my sins, and come into my heart and be my Lord and Savior," and the signature of heaven will be on your adoption papers for eternity. Devil, we are giving you an eviction notice.

My brothers and sisters around the world, pray these prayers with me so that in the name of Jesus Christ we can stop people from falling off the cliff. Let's speak these words and shame the devil and the systems of the world.

Today I declare over the church at large that I break every fragmented and every compromised spirit. Let them be destroyed and removed from the house of God by the blood of Jesus. In Jesus' mighty name, amen.

Let every evil seed that was planted in the house of God rot, shrivel up, and die, in Jesus' mighty name.

Let every demonic, counterfeit preaching of the Word of God and every counterfeit teaching of the Word of God be uprooted and removed from the house of God today, in the name of Jesus Christ. Amen.

I declare and decree right now that the Bible, the true Word of God, will be preached completely, fully, and uncompromised, from Genesis to Revelation, in the house of the Lord forever. In Jesus' mighty name, amen.

I smite, uproot, and put the judgment of God upon every wicked and demonic lukewarm, delusional, compromising, and delirious spirit that has crept into the house of God. Let the fire of the Holy Spirit burn them all out from the north, the east, the west, and the south today.

Let the Holy Spirit by His fire purify, cleanse, and baptize the church once again in the blood of Jesus, completely and fully, and forevermore. In Jesus' unmatchable name, amen.

Chapter 12

THE BOOK THE DEVIL HATES

THERE IS A reason the devil hates the Word of God with everything he's got. Let me share the story of Lazarus with you:

So Jesus, again being deeply moved within, came to the tomb. Now it was a cave, and a stone was lying against it. Jesus said, "Remove the stone." Martha, the sister of the deceased, said to Him, "Lord, by this time there will be a stench, for he has been dead four days." Jesus said to her, "Did I not say to you that if you believe, you will see the glory of God?" So they removed the stone. And Jesus raised His eyes, and said, "Father, I thank You that You have heard Me. But I knew that You always hear Me; nevertheless, because of the people standing around I said it, so that they may believe that You sent Me." And when He had said these things, He cried out with a loud voice, "Lazarus, come out!" Out came the man who had died, bound hand and foot with wrappings, and his face was wrapped around with a cloth. Jesus said to them, "Unbind him, and let him go."

—JOHN 11:38–44, NASB

Dead People Walking: It's Time to Live

It has been said that Jesus didn't come to make bad people good; He came to make dead people alive. The devil knows this, because death is in his playbook. The devil hates the Bible more than any other book on the entire planet because he knows the Bible makes you alive. He knows the Word of God will loose you from your tormentors and unbind you from your dirty past and your mistakes. The Bible will set you free to live the life that God has for you.

When Lazarus came out of the tomb, he couldn't see, he couldn't walk, he couldn't dance, and he couldn't talk. He was immobile. I'll say it again: Jesus didn't come to make bad people good; He came to make dead people alive. Our story is a Lazarus story.

Christianity is a resurrection from the dead. Before salvation, we were physically alive but spiritually dead.

When He raised Lazarus from the dead, Jesus told the people to remove the stone and take off Lazarus' graveclothes. This shows us Jesus will always do His part, but He will never do yours. "I do My part," the Lord says, "and I will tell you what I expect you to do."

Many of us assume that our emotions and feelings tell us what God expects us to do. I think nine out of ten times we miss it. God expects you to read your Bible, to make it your best friend. That's why we need Jesus in order to be alive. That's why we need the Bible; it's the oxygen that keeps us alive. The devil hates the Bible. Christianity is a resurrection from the dead. Jesus came to make dead people alive.

When the devil tries to distract you, make it personal. Tell him to his face, "Satan, listen to me. You're going to loose me now. Get your hands off me in the name of Jesus. I will make the Bible, the book that you hate with all your heart, my best friend." It's not just about reading the Bible. It's about loving the Bible. The devil doesn't mind if you read it; he just doesn't want you to love it.

Second Corinthians 4:16 (NASB) says, "Therefore we do not lose heart, but though our outer person is decaying, yet our inner person is being renewed day by day." That's why the devil fights so hard to stop you from parking yourself in front of the Bible. Even if your outer man is falling off the hinges and you're getting old, your inner man is being renewed every day because the Bible is the spiritual oxygen that it needs. The devil is trying to cut off your oxygen.

A. W. Tozer, speaking of the believer, said it like this: "He dies so he can live, forsakes in order to have, gives away so he can keep, sees the invisible, hears the inaudible and knows that which passeth knowledge."[1]

Jesus has given us His Word, the Bible, as a gift on a silver platter. You have to catch this. When you make the Bible your best friend, something amazing happens. A. W. Tozer also said, "A real Christian is an odd number anyway. He feels supreme love for One whom he has never seen, talks familiarly every day to Someone he cannot see, expects to go to heaven on the virtue of Another."[2] Man, that's good! You get all that from the Word of God. It's no wonder the devil hates the Bible. Say it with me: "Devil, how do you like them apples?"

When we read the Word of God and make it our best friend, we will not lose heart in any battle. The Bible is more than just a book. Read 2 Corinthians 4:16–18 (NASB); this is what happens for the believer: "Therefore we do not lose heart, but though our outer person is decaying, yet our inner person is being renewed day by day. For our momentary, light affliction is producing for us an eternal weight of glory far beyond all comparison, while we look not at the things which are seen, but at the things which are not seen; for the things which are seen are temporal, but the things which are not seen are eternal."

There is a warning sign about this in the devil's playbook. The devil says, "Keep them away from the Bible. Keep them away from their oxygen tank because good things happen for those who make the Bible their everything."

That's why the devil has worked so hard to take the Bible out of many churches today. He has taken the Word of God out of the house of God. My question to the church at large is, How are you capable of losing God's book in God's house? What a spiritual tragedy.

The devil has also used this tactic against many believers around the world. If the enemy can take the Bible out of our homes, he can keep us running on empty and looking to man-made inventions to replace the ultimate book. The Bible has been a bestseller for nearly five hundred years, and the devil is angry.

When believers in the underground churches in China get a suitcase full of Bibles, they cry like babies. I've seen videos. A person can get killed for carrying a Bible in North Korea, China, and other places because the devil hates the Bible. But many of us in America have five Bibles at home and don't even touch one. It's crazy.

I heard an amazing story about 9/11, when that horrific tragedy happened in New York City. There were two precious sisters in one of the buildings. I don't remember which floor they were on, but they took the stairs to escape the burning building, quoting Psalm 23 the whole way down. There was an unbeliever behind them, right on their heels, repeating the words of Psalm 23.

When the news media interviewed the unbeliever a few days

later, the man had memorized Psalm 23 completely. The Word of God is alive, and you can't deny it. Even as an unbeliever this man didn't cry out for his family, for fame, or for Citibank; he cried out for the Word of God to save him that day.

In the heart of Washington, DC, not far from the US Capitol, the White House, and the Washington Monument, there is a beautiful building housing the Museum of the Bible. The history portrayed in that building is amazing. It is the history of sacrifices, of people who have suffered for the Bible throughout the centuries. It tells the stories of amazing people like William Tyndale, John Wycliffe, Johannes Gutenberg, Martin Luther, and other men and women of God who preserved, protected, and even died for the Bible so that you and I can hold the precious Word of God in our hands and in our hearts today.

Don't take the Word of God for granted. It is powerful, and people sacrificed so much throughout history so you could read it for yourself. This is a hallelujah moment. It's time to set your course to chase after the Bible, the Word of God. Jesus Himself showed us the power of the Word of God when He used it to destroy the devil. The Bible fights, and the Bible ignites.

It Is Written; It's Over, Devil

Do you remember the story of the devil tempting Jesus in the wilderness that we talked about earlier? That is what the devil does. He tried to tempt Jesus, and he will try to tempt you. He wants you to take a shortcut and bypass God's Word. He wants you to create your own path instead of following the path outlined in the Word of God.

When the devil tried to set Jesus up for a downfall in the wilderness by twisting Psalm 91, Jesus hit him so hard with the Word that the devil forgot his birthday. Things got even crazier when the devil showed Jesus the splendors of the world and said, "If you bow down to me and worship me, I'll give you these." (See Matthew 4:8–9.)

Think about it—how crazy is that? The devil makes offers for your soul hoping you will take the bait instead of waiting on God for His blessings and His very best. The devil was offering Jesus the splendors of the world, but look at Revelation 11:15 (NASB): "The kingdom of the world has become the kingdom of our Lord and of His Christ; and He will reign forever and ever." The devil was trying to rob Jesus, but Jesus beat him down with the Word.

That's why the devil has stolen the Bible, the Word of God, from the house of God and from churches around the world. He is clever. He knows a Wordless Christian is a powerless Christian. Thank God there is a remnant of believers who can't live without the Word, our spiritual oxygen.

Listen carefully, my brothers and sisters, to the words of Josh McDowell: "When it comes to my salvation, all I need is Jesus; after my salvation, everything is Jesus plus the church."[3] In other words, Jesus is all you need to be saved, but once you are saved, you need Jesus plus a real church that is preaching the Word of God.

I'll also say this: Jesus left His church to complete His mission on the earth. As Charles Spurgeon said, "The Church is the world's hope."[4] How can we give the world hope without the Bible?

I hear Christians today ask the million-dollar question: Can I be a Christian without going to church? To these people I say, "Keep it simple. Yes, you can be a Christian, but not a growing Christian."

A. W. Tozer said, "Whatever keeps me from the Bible is my enemy, however harmless it may appear to be."[5] The Bible is not just a book. The devil knows that his playbook is made useless by the Word of God. Remember, the Bible fights, and the Bible ignites.

HEAR TWO VOICES, OBEY ONE

Hear these words the apostle Paul spoke under the unction of the Holy Spirit: "Take the helmet of salvation and the sword of the Spirit, which is the word of God" (Eph. 6:17). How does the Word of God become a weapon?

These are not just words on a page that the devil wants you not to believe. In Matthew 4, Jesus gave us the ultimate, most powerful teaching on how to use the Word, the sword of the Spirit, against the enemy of your soul. The devil has a PhD in distorting God's Word. He takes away the sharpness of God's Word when he distorts it in your mind.

People, wake up. This is powerful spiritual teaching straight out of the devil's playbook. Many people want "Boom! Bang!" theology. But we don't want to be like firecrackers—a big bang that produces nothing. When the devil twists the Word of God, he tries to send you the wrong way and put you into the wrong timing for your purpose and your destiny. Our blessings come straight from the Word of God, the Bible. Let's not stay spiritually ignorant.

I think it's off the hook that right before Jesus went into the wilderness, "a voice from the heavens said, 'This is My beloved Son, with whom I am well pleased'" (Matt. 3:17, NASB). My precious brothers and sisters, pay attention to this on a spiritual level. In any battle in any season, right after God speaks to you, Satan will speak too. I will prove this to you straight from the Word of God. The Father sealed the deal by saying, "This is my beloved Son, with whom I'm well pleased," and only three verses later we find the devil telling Jesus, "If You are the Son of God, command that these stones become bread" (Matt. 4:3, NASB).

Think about that. Meditate on it. Right after Jesus heard a voice from heaven say, "This is my beloved Son, with whom I am well pleased," the devil brought a basketful of question marks, saying, "If you are the Son of God..." Man, that sounds pretty familiar to me. There is nothing new in the devil's kingdom. This crony, this loser, this counterfeit only knows how to rewrap his old hogwash. He said pretty much the same thing to Adam and Eve in Genesis 3:1 (NASB): "Has God really said, 'You shall not eat from any tree of the garden'?"

Have you noticed that when you're at a crossroads or on the battlefield, the devil will bring questions to your mind like "Did God really say this?" or "Are you truly a Christian?" He tries to fill you with doubt and unbelief and put question marks on your purpose and your destiny to take you out of the battle.

I tell you right now, my brothers and sisters, it's time to get strapped. You need to be armed and dangerous. Put on your holster and put the ultimate weapon—the Bible—into it. The only way we can fight the voice of the devil and hell is through the Word of God. The Bible is boot camp for the true believer. It's the oxygen that keeps the inner man going—it's better than the Energizer bunny.

A Bible in the hands of the believer brings freedom, and that is why the devil tries to keep the Word of God away from you today. Jesus said, "If you continue in My word, then you are truly My disciples; and you will know the truth, and the truth will set you free" (John 8:31–32, NASB). No Bible, no freedom.

Give God your time. Spend time abiding in His Word. That is our weapon of mass destruction. The devil doesn't want you to understand how effective of a weapon God's Word really is.

When we abide in the Word, God's presence becomes tangible to us, and the Bible becomes more than just a book.

It's time for believers to turn the tables on the devil and put him underfoot once and for all. The devil hates the Bible, and he especially hates when we develop a passion, a love, a hunger, and a thirst for the Word of God.

Pray these prayers with me, and start living in freedom through the Word of God:

> *Let the power of the blood of Jesus be released upon pastors, leaders, evangelists, teachers, and prophets of the house of God completely and fully through the Word of God, in Jesus' mighty name.*
>
> *Let every demon's strategy against my brothers and sisters who are trying to go higher and deeper with the Lord Jesus Christ in the Word of God this year be drowned in the blood of Jesus.*
>
> *I draw a line of protection around myself, my family, my house, and my ministry. I pray that my eyes will be open, my ears will be open, and my heart will be open and receptive to the Word of God. As for me and my house, we will serve Jesus Christ. Amen.*
>
> *Let every satanic operation that is trying to steal the Word of God out of my life be destroyed completely and fully.*
>
> *I release the vengeance of the Holy Spirit upon every wicked spirit that is trying to steal my time in the Word of God and the revelation and clarity that I need*

to walk in the truth, from Genesis to Revelation, in Jesus' name. Amen.

Let every power of darkness that is trying to frustrate me and stop me from reading the Word of the Lord and spending time in my Bible drown in the blood of Jesus. Amen.

I destroy and uproot out of my prayer closet right now every devil that is trying to steal my time and my moments with God. I frustrate the plans of the devil; I paralyze them, and I uproot them out of my prayer closet. Whether it's the church, my home, or my loved ones, we will stand in unity and in awe of the power of the Holy Spirit to heal every place that the devil has fragmented in order to steal our time in prayer, in the Word, and in God's presence. We drown those devils and their demonic and satanic operations completely and fully in the blood of Jesus. Amen.

Chapter 13

THE UNSEEN GOD

ANY OF US miss seeing the providence of God today in our daily lives, our prayer lives, and our Bible times because the devil doesn't want us to receive or spiritually comprehend the concept. It's crazy how many times even in the simplicity of life we complain, murmur, or get mad. We get angry when we get in a traffic jam, when we get stuck in an airport, when a meeting is canceled, or when bad weather kicks in and we can't leave the house. Somehow we think that the devil has ruined our day.

We get quick-tempered and distressed in these situations, and our emotions run ninety miles an hour. But what we do not realize is that God is behind every episode, every moment, and every detail of our lives, protecting us and guiding us in His perfect timing through everything that happens, every day.

We miss it. Because of that traffic jam, God stopped your car from being in an accident. That delay at the airport, when you sat there for three hours, stopped the plane from being involved in a crash. I remember how upset and disappointed I would get when I had delays at the airport at the beginning of my ministry—but then I realized the big picture. Now when I'm at the airport for six hours due to a delay, I'm calm, rejoicing, and thanking God for it. Even the simplest things, like when someone cuts you off or skips the line and you think, "How rude!" or "How disrespectful!" are the providence of God at work.

We let the devil trigger us. We allow the enemy to confuse us and rob us spiritually blind, leaving us unable to see God's unseen hand at work in our lives. That's what this chapter is about. I don't want you to miss Him, the unseen God, in every detail and situation of your life.

The Corrupt Words of the Evil One

How many times the devil has stolen those moments from us, the providence of a mighty God. It's amazing how God can do something in your life, and then you steal the glory from His name because you are quick to be worldly. This is in the enemy's playbook.

Listen to this carefully with your spiritual ears: if chance or good luck exists, then God doesn't exist. The existence of chance and luck would mean there are things that God doesn't control. I want you to sit with that for a moment and let it hit your spirit. When we bring up words like *chance*, *luck*, *happenstance*, *wish*, and *wishing* in our spiritual vocabulary, we take away from who God is in our lives. We mock the providence of God. We give the devil the glory because those are his words, straight out of his demonic, despicable playbook.

Those words are sent from the heart of the enemy to rob you of your ability to see the hand of God in your life. God is sovereign. He controls everything, every day, all day. Why are you letting the devil rob you of the providence of God, who holds the pen of your story?

Read these powerful words by J. C. Ryle: "Nothing whatever, whether great or small, can happen to a believer, without God's ordering and permission....There is no such thing as 'chance,' 'luck,' or 'accident' in the Christian's journey through this world."[1]

It's time to wake up spiritually, my brothers and sisters. Stop allowing the devil to distort the providence of God in your life. Words like *chance, luck, accident,* and *coincidence* don't bless the Lord; they don't glorify Him, and they don't edify you. Using these words takes away from God's day-to-day involvement in your life, so why would you choose to believe and agree with the devil?

Many times in our journeys with the Lord Jesus Christ, His providence goes unseen and unnoticed because the devil has robbed us of our ability to see the unseen hand of God. God is always moving in our lives. Psalm 46:1 says, "God is our refuge and strength, an ever-present help in trouble." J. C. Ryle said, "All is arranged and appointed by God. And all things are 'working together' for the believer's good (Rom. 8:28)."[2]

THE FINGERPRINTS OF GOD

Listen to me, my brothers and sisters. Let me keep it real with you. God's day-to-day involvement in your life is called His providence. Providence is God's involvement in and orchestration of every day and every place in your life. Providence reminds us that every detail is carefully managed by God, and it thereby disqualifies coincidence and chance, which we already learned come from the devil's playbook.

Derek Thomas wrote, "God loves details! It is in the details that we discern his hand of providence—ruling, directing, providing, sustaining, preventing, surprising. What may look catastrophic from one point of view will appear from another angle to be the outworking of a plan in which God is in full control."[3] What an awesome God we serve.

We honor God when we remove words like *luck*, *good fortune*, and *coincidence* from our spiritual language and instead describe every event as God's providence or His hand orchestrating and demonstrating His love toward you and me. We shame the devil when we say, "I'm not lucky. I don't have good fortune. I'm in Christ."

Words like *chance* and *luck* have no place in my head, my mouth, or my heart. I'm in Christ. That should be your story. Don't let the devil steal it from you. You do not just happen to be in the right place at the right time. You are in Christ, which means you are in the right place in Him. My prayer for you, right in the middle of the chapter, is that you will put these words in your heart. Trusting God's providence means believing that He can use a string of seemingly unrelated events to accomplish His purpose and will in your life. That's a good prayer to stand on.

Listen carefully. Some of the things you are going through look like they came out of nowhere or happened by accident. Hold up! That's what the devil wants you to think. He wants to confuse you and blind you spiritually so you won't discern the unseen hand of God in your season, your trial, your tribulation, or your testing. All these things prove Romans 8:28, which says, "And we know that in all things God works for the good of those who love him, who have been called according to his purpose."

God Is Always in Control—All Day, Every Day

Let me now share a testimony with you from my own life to show you that God controls everything, including time, and lives in eternity, but He will step into time to move in your life and mine at any given time, and the devil can do nothing about it.

This is how my story goes. In 1997, I got a revelation out of nowhere that I wasn't being a good father to my daughter. I was in the demonic world. I caught flashbacks and remembered how when she was two years old she would sit by the window waiting for her daddy because I'd promised her the day before that I would pick her up and take her to the park. I was a no-show. I felt guilt and shame as a devil worshipper with a demonic mindset and a demonic heart.

I was a despicable person, sinner of all sinners, living in the shadows of the demonic. I owed the devil and his kingdom my life, and I worked like a workhorse to promote and advance the dark side like no other human being. And all the while I was breaking my little daughter's heart as she stood by the window waiting for her dad to take her to the park, for a bike ride, or to get ice cream, but I never showed up. Her mother would call me and say, "Your daughter was in tears by the window hoping you'd show up." And I had no emotions about those things.

But in 1997, I got hit hard. I wondered, "Why am I not a good dad to my daughter?" My daughter was a little older then, and I wanted to make up for some lost time. I asked the devil for permission to take a sabbatical from witchcraft, and the answer was no.

I told the devil, "I'm taking it anyway. I don't care what you have to say."

So I quit. During that time, I got hit with a punishment. Out of nowhere I had a retinal detachment. I went to my contact center, where I got my glasses and contacts, and the man told me, "There's something wrong with the back of your eye. You don't need contacts; you need to see an eye specialist."

He sent me over to the hospital, and as soon as they saw me they said, "Tomorrow morning you need surgery." I wasn't sure what they were talking about because I'd had the condition for two weeks. They told me, "Because of the grace of God you haven't lost your eyesight. Your retina is detached. That means that the wallpaper in the back of your eye is down so you can't see."

The devil punished me, and I had to have major surgery. I was blind for one year, but I still couldn't see my daughter. In the middle of that year I prayed to the dark side to give me back my eyesight and forgive me for my disrespect.

A year later, in 1998, my eyesight came back, and I gave the devil all the credit and props. Now that I could see again, I dove into the deep of the dark side, going even deeper and becoming more fervent and more attentive to the demonic than ever before. I felt that I was on good terms with the devil and the demons and owed them respect for giving me back my eyesight.

In 1999 I went to hell and came back. I died in my apartment, went to hell as a satanic warlock, and came back as a believer in Christ.

A couple years later I heard the voice of the Lord in my spirit. He asked me, "Do you remember when you lost your eyesight?"

I said, "Yes, I do remember, Lord."

He said, "You were praising the devil, and you were giving the devil his respect for giving you back the eyesight. Little did you know, and little do you know, it was Me that gave you your eyesight because I have a plan and a purpose for your life. I have called you to be an evangelist and destroy the works of darkness with My name. I was the One that restored your eyesight."

That is the providence of God, the unseen hand of God. When He shows up, unseen and unnoticed, He is so good, so merciful, and so loving.

When I was in the depths of hell with no eyesight, God was thinking of me, and He blessed me and restored my eyesight. He took the pen out of the devil's hand to start writing my story in

1999. That's why I love God so much and am sold out to Him. That's why I always say, "I'm doing life in Jesus with no parole. I'm on death row. I owe Him everything. He owes me nothing."

That's what I'm trying to explain about the providence of God. I thought it was the devil who gave me back my eyesight. I thought it was good luck or good fortune or coincidence. No; it was God. It was the unseen hand of His mercy upon my life. And I'm sure the same has happened for you hundreds or even thousands of times. We have missed it. But we're going to stop today. We're going to punch the devil in the face. We aren't going to miss it anymore.

From this day forward we will have eyes to see and ears to hear our Lord Jesus Christ, who is going to show us the providence of God—His goodness, His mercy, and His grace upon our lives. God has something more for us. He is involved in the details of our lives, both in the good times and in the difficult times. By coincidence? By chance? No way. It's providence. God is working out His plan for my life and yours. So start calling it by the right name: providence.

Proverbs 18:21 says, "The tongue has the power of life and death, and those who love it will eat its fruit." Nothing happens by luck, chance, good fortune, or an accident. Take those words out of your head and out of your mouth, and crush the devil's playbook. Let's shut it down and shut him up. We honor God, not Satan. We honor God when we remove these words from our spiritual language.

I'm not lucky; I'm in Christ. Sometimes when I share my testimony people say, "Oh, you're so lucky. You're so lucky because David Wilkerson was your spiritual father. You're so lucky that you went to Times Square Church." No, I'm not. It's the hand of God over my life. I'm kicking the devil in the head and exposing his demonic playbook. He has tried to make Christians so comfortable with stealing and robbing God's glory and the provident hand of God in their lives that they call it the norm—but I'm exposing that. We are not lucky; we are in Christ.

God's providence also involves Him connecting the spiritual dots in our lives. Even when our circumstances seem radical, crazy, and out of place, God is connecting the spiritual dots. God knows the beginning and the end of everything, including your story. God sits in the place where the devil can't sit, and His providence will sustain us. Period.

GOD'S TIMING IS ALWAYS PERFECT; DON'T MISS IT

The Book of Acts speaks about a great persecution, and it also speaks about the Great Commission. What, if anything, do a great persecution and the Great Commission have in common? Let's look at some crazy events from Acts chapter 8:

> Now Saul was consenting to his death. At that time a great persecution arose against the church which was at Jerusalem; and they were all scattered throughout the regions of Judea and Samaria, except the apostles. And devout men carried Stephen to his burial, and made great lamentation over him. As for Saul, he made havoc of the church, entering every house, and dragging off men and women, committing them to prison. Therefore, those who were scattered went everywhere preaching the word.
>
> —ACTS 8:1–4, NKJV

When these things were happening, everything seemed to be upside down. It looked like everything was out of control. There was a great persecution, and people were scattered everywhere.

But look at two words from this passage: *Judea* and *Samaria.* Don't miss them.

Now, read Acts 1:8 (NKJV) and look at the hand and providence of God: "But you shall receive power when the Holy Spirit has come upon you; and you shall be witnesses to Me in Jerusalem, and in all Judea and Samaria, and to the end of the earth." There you go. In Acts 1:8, God gave His word; then in Acts 8:1–4, persecution broke out to fulfill Jesus' commission that His followers would preach in Judea and Samaria. Catch this in your spirit. God said it, and the mission was accomplished because of persecution. And don't miss the fact that this crazy man, this loony tune, this madman named Saul who was in the midst of all the upside-down craziness of Acts 8:1–4 later became the great apostle Paul. God is good.

When things seem crazy, out of place, and upside down in your life, remember it's the providence of God working all things out for you because you love Him. Don't quit, don't give up, and don't make permanent decisions in the middle of temporary situations. Let the hand of God move upon your life. What seems to be a problem can actually be the providence of God, so remember, "Be still, and know that I am God; I will be exalted among the nations, I will be exalted in the earth!" (Ps. 46:10, NKJV). Amen.

The prophet Isaiah said, "For as the heavens are higher than the earth, so are My ways higher than your ways, and My thoughts than your thoughts" (Isa. 55:9, NKJV). God uses seemingly unrelated events to accomplish His purpose in your life. So nothing that happens to you is the result of good luck, good fortune, chance, happenstance, or coincidence; God doesn't exist in those words. What seems to be spiritually crazy is actually the providence of God, His unseen hand working it out, doing His thing, showing that He is God and the devil is not. The devil doesn't want you to know this, so he tries to keep you from comprehending it. But that ends today.

We're going to burn up the devil's playbook with the fire of the Holy Spirit. From now on we will recognize the providence of God and know these are spiritual nuggets, spiritual understandings, spiritual teachings straight out of heaven. Jesus is writing a greater story about you. Nothing is coincidence or happenstance; that's the devil whispering in your ear. We're getting the spiritual cotton swab and cleaning your ears out, in Jesus' name.

Think about this: How did the gospel get to Africa? By chance? By coincidence? By luck? No, by the providence of God.

Philip, a deacon in the church, was preaching and having a revival in Samaria. Even Simon the sorcerer got baptized. But then Philip got some new instructions:

> Now an angel of the Lord spoke to Philip, saying, "Arise and go toward the south along the road which goes down from Jerusalem to Gaza." This is desert. So he arose and went. And behold, a man of Ethiopia, a eunuch of great authority under Candace the queen of the Ethiopians, who had charge of all her treasury, and had come to Jerusalem to worship, was returning. And sitting in his chariot, he was reading Isaiah the prophet. Then the Spirit said to Philip, "Go near and overtake this chariot."
>
> So Philip ran to him, and heard him reading the prophet Isaiah, and said, "Do you understand what you are reading?"
> And he said, "How can I, unless someone guides me?" And he asked Philip to come up and sit with him. The place in the Scripture which he read was this: "He was led as a sheep to the slaughter; and as a lamb before its shearer is silent, so He opened not His mouth. In His humiliation His justice was taken away, and who will declare His generation? For His life is taken from the earth."

So the eunuch answered Philip and said, "I ask you, of whom does the prophet say this, of himself or of some other man?" Then Philip opened his mouth, and beginning at this Scripture, preached Jesus to him. Now as they went down the road, they came to some water. And the eunuch said, "See, here is water. What hinders me from being baptized?"

Then Philip said, "If you believe with all your heart, you may."

And he answered and said, "I believe that Jesus Christ is the Son of God."

So he commanded the chariot to stand still. And both Philip and the eunuch went down into the water, and he baptized him. Now when they came up out of the water, the Spirit of the Lord caught Philip away, so that the eunuch saw him no more; and he went on his way rejoicing. But Philip was found at Azotus. And passing through, he preached in all the cities till he came to Caesarea.

—ACTS 8:26–40, NKJV

Wow! What a coincidence. Boy, that man was lucky that Philip showed up out of nowhere. Boy, he must have good fortune. By chance. Circumstance. By accident.

The devil is a liar. The providence of God took Philip from Samaria and put him on a desert road in the right place at the right time to speak to this man, and this man brought the gospel to Africa. God in His providence was moving His unseen hand to accomplish His purpose. "So we are convinced that every detail of our lives is continually woven together for good, for we are his lovers who have been called to fulfill his designed purpose" (Rom. 8:28, TPT).

Stop agreeing with the devil. Providence is the hidden hand of God. If you were born in the projects, that's God's doing. If you were born into a crazy family, that's God doing. If you were born in poverty, that's God's doing. If you were born on a mountaintop or in Beverly Hills, that's God's doing. He works all things out for those who believe, trust, and put their faith in Him (Rom. 8:28). "Heaven rules" (Dan. 4:26, NKJV), so God expects us to "fix our eyes not on what is seen, but on what is unseen, since what is seen is temporary, but what is unseen is eternal" (2 Cor. 4:18).

I don't want you to miss this, brothers and sisters. This is spiritual warfare at its best. These are spiritual nuggets. When the devil robs you of something that belongs to God, he is engaging in spiritual warfare. If you don't want to get robbed by the enemy, then you need these teachings to equip you, to empower you, and to help you open your spiritual eyes so you can see the unseen hand of God moving on your behalf. That is what this book is all about, from beginning to end.

The devil is robbing us today, and he's laughing all the way to the spiritual bank. He's laughing because no one is teaching and equipping the saints or giving us the spiritual nuggets we need to go deeper and further and see the enemy of our souls coming to steal what God has blessed us with. We're napping. We should be up and ready, armed and dangerous, but instead we're snoring.

Consider Romans 11:33: "Oh, the depth of the riches both of the wisdom and knowledge of God! How unsearchable are His judgments and His ways past finding out!" (NKJV). How awesome is that!

Duncan Campbell said, "The kingdom of God is not going to be advanced by our churches becoming filled with men, but by men in our churches becoming filled with God."[4] Let's stop filling the churches of God with people and instead fill the people in the church with God. We're losing the fight; we're wasting our time filling the house of God with people. That's what the devil wants.

Do you remember the story of the woman at the well? A Samaritan woman came to draw water in the middle of the day, and Jesus was at the well. He asked her for a drink of water, but in the end, she was introduced to the living water. She met the Messiah, Jesus Christ. "The woman then left her waterpot, went her way into the city, and said to the men, 'Come, see a Man who told me all things that I ever did. Could this be the Christ?' Then they went out of the city and came to Him" (John 4:28–30, NKJV).

What an amazing coincidence. What good luck that woman had. By chance, good fortune came her way. Hogwash! That's a lie of the enemy. Jesus Christ is so amazing. He's so awesome. Out of all the wells in Samaria, Jesus sat at the right one at the right time. He spoke to this precious woman who was hungry and thirsty, and He put aside His own physical thirst to take care of her spiritual thirst.

The provident hand of God was at work at that moment, and this woman became a great evangelist. She went into her town and spoke to the people, and she brought the entire town to the feet of Jesus. What a moment! That was not a coincidence; that was God. I thank God that He doesn't show favoritism. He can use anyone, man or woman, at any given time. All you have to do is say, "Here am I, Lord. Use me." Amen.

LET YOUR STORY BE A TESTIMONY

I end this chapter with the incredible story of Joseph, who was falsely accused, betrayed by his brothers, and sold into slavery at the age of seventeen—but God had given him a promise.

> Then the butler and the baker of the king of Egypt, who were confined in the prison, had a dream, both of them,

each man's dream in one night and each man's dream with its own interpretation. And Joseph came in to them in the morning and looked at them, and saw that they were sad. So he asked Pharaoh's officers who were with him in the custody of his lord's house, saying, "Why do you look so sad today?"

And they said to him, "We each have had a dream, and there is no interpreter of it."

So Joseph said to them, "Do not interpretations belong to God? Tell them to me, please."

Then the chief butler told his dream to Joseph, and said to him, "Behold, in my dream a vine was before me, and in the vine were three branches; it was as though it budded, its blossoms shot forth, and its clusters brought forth ripe grapes. Then Pharaoh's cup was in my hand; and I took the grapes and pressed them into Pharaoh's cup, and placed the cup in Pharaoh's hand."

And Joseph said to him, "This is the interpretation of it: The three branches are three days. Now within three days Pharaoh will lift up your head and restore you to your place, and you will put Pharaoh's cup in his hand according to the former manner, when you were his butler. But remember me when it is well with you, and please show kindness to me; make mention of me to Pharaoh, and get me out of this house. For indeed I was stolen away from the land of the Hebrews; and also I have done nothing here that they should put me into the dungeon."

When the chief baker saw that the interpretation was good, he said to Joseph, "I also was in my dream, and there were three white baskets on my head. In the uppermost basket were all kinds of baked goods for Pharaoh, and the birds ate them out of the basket on my head."

So Joseph answered and said, "This is the interpretation

of it: The three baskets are three days. Within three days Pharaoh will lift off your head from you and hang you on a tree; and the birds will eat your flesh from you."

—GENESIS 40:5–19, NKJV

Sometime later, because he had correctly interpreted the dreams of Pharaoh's officers in prison, Joseph ended up in front of Pharaoh himself to interpret his dream.

> Now it came to pass in the morning that his spirit was troubled, and he sent and called for all the magicians of Egypt and all its wise men. And Pharaoh told them his dreams, but there was no one who could interpret them for Pharaoh.
>
> Then the chief butler spoke to Pharaoh, saying: "I remember my faults this day. When Pharaoh was angry with his servants, and put me in custody in the house of the captain of the guard, both me and the chief baker, we each had a dream in one night, he and I. Each of us dreamed according to the interpretation of his own dream. Now there was a young Hebrew man with us there, a servant of the captain of the guard. And we told him, and he interpreted our dreams for us; to each man he interpreted according to his own dream. And it came to pass, just as he interpreted for us, so it happened. He restored me to my office, and he hanged him."
>
> Then Pharaoh sent and called Joseph, and they brought him quickly out of the dungeon; and he shaved, changed his clothing, and came to Pharaoh. And Pharaoh said to Joseph, "I have had a dream, and there is no one who can interpret it. But I have heard it said of you that you can understand a dream, to interpret it."
>
> So Joseph answered Pharaoh, saying, "It is not in me; God will give Pharaoh an answer of peace."
>
> Then Pharaoh said to Joseph: "Behold, in my dream I

stood on the bank of the river. Suddenly seven cows came up out of the river, fine looking and fat; and they fed in the meadow. Then behold, seven other cows came up after them, poor and very ugly and gaunt, such ugliness as I have never seen in all the land of Egypt. And the gaunt and ugly cows ate up the first seven, the fat cows. When they had eaten them up, no one would have known that they had eaten them, for they were just as ugly as at the beginning. So I awoke. Also I saw in my dream, and suddenly seven heads came up on one stalk, full and good. Then behold, seven heads, withered, thin, and blighted by the east wind, sprang up after them. And the thin heads devoured the seven good heads. So I told this to the magicians, but there was no one who could explain it to me."

Then Joseph said to Pharaoh, "The dreams of Pharaoh are one; God has shown Pharaoh what He is about to do: The seven good cows are seven years, and the seven good heads are seven years; the dreams are one. And the seven thin and ugly cows which came up after them are seven years, and the seven empty heads blighted by the east wind are seven years of famine. This is the thing which I have spoken to Pharaoh. God has shown Pharaoh what He is about to do. Indeed seven years of great plenty will come throughout all the land of Egypt; but after them seven years of famine will arise, and all the plenty will be forgotten in the land of Egypt; and the famine will deplete the land. So the plenty will not be known in the land because of the famine following, for it will be very severe. And the dream was repeated to Pharaoh twice because the thing is established by God, and God will shortly bring it to pass."

—Genesis 41:8–32, NKJV

In response, this is what Pharaoh did for Joseph:

So the advice was good in the eyes of Pharaoh and in the eyes of all his servants. And Pharaoh said to his servants, "Can we find such a one as this, a man in whom is the Spirit of God?"

Then Pharaoh said to Joseph, "Inasmuch as God has shown you all this, there is no one as discerning and wise as you. You shall be over my house, and all my people shall be ruled according to your word; only in regard to the throne will I be greater than you." And Pharaoh said to Joseph, "See, I have set you over all the land of Egypt."

—Genesis 41:37–41, NKJV

Wow! If Joseph hadn't known his God—the God of Israel; the God of Abraham, Isaac, and Jacob; the God we serve today—he probably would have said, "I'm a lucky man. What a coincidence. I have good fortune. What a chance that this good thing would happen for me!" He would have spoken all these worldly, demonic words. But when the devil turned Joseph's world upside down, providence—the hand of God—was connecting the dots to get Joseph to Pharaoh and promote him and bless him so God could bring His people to the land of Egypt.

God always has a plan and a purpose. He's always in control. The providence of the King of kings and Lord of lords rules over your life and mine, forever and ever, in Jesus' mighty, unmatchable name. Amen.

It's time for us to take the devil out. Pray these arsenal prayers with me:

Let every satanic seed that was planted in my eyes, in my mind, and in my heart in order to keep me from seeing God's providence be ripped out, destroyed, and uprooted in my life, in Jesus' name. Amen.

I dip my mind, my eyes, and my heart in the blood of Jesus. I will not miss any moment or any opportunity to experience an open heaven in my life, in Jesus' mighty name.

I declare and decree now that the blood of Jesus will destroy every satanic gathering that is working against me in the spirit realm; destroy every hindrance, delay, and blockage; and destroy every plot, scheme, and wile today that is stopping me from seeing the providence of God, the unseen hand of my Lord and Savior in my life, in the unmatchable name of Jesus Christ. Amen.

Every witchcraft altar that is trying to steal, kill, and destroy the providence of God, the unseen hand of God, and every God moment in the spirit over me, my family, my loved ones, my ministry, my purpose, and my destiny will drown completely and fully today in the blood of Jesus, never to rise up again. In Jesus' awesome, mighty, all-powerful name I pray. Amen.

NOTES

CHAPTER 2

1. "About the Formula 409 Brand," Formula 409, accessed May 18, 2024, https://www.formula409.com/about-us/formula-409/.

CHAPTER 3

1. "Learning to Stop Before It's Too Late," The 260 Journey, October 5, 2021, https://www.listennotes.com/podcasts/the-260-journey/learning-to-stop-before-its-amoXQb3LIVp/.
2. *Merriam-Webster*, s.v. "temptation," accessed May 6, 2024, https://www.merriam-webster.com/dictionary/temptation.
3. R. A. Torrey and Edward D. Andrews, *Christian Living: How to Succeed in the Christian Life* (Cambridge, OH: Christian Publishing House, 2023), 201, https://www.google.com/books/edition/CHRISTIAN_LIVING/X9nVDAAAQBAJ?hl=en&gbpv=1.
4. Charles H. Spurgeon, "Evening, February 20," *Morning and Evening: Daily Readings*, accessed May 6, 2024, https://www.ccel.org/ccel/spurgeon/morneve.d0220pm.html.

CHAPTER 4

1. "The Nicene Creed" (contemporary version), Book of Common Prayer Online, accessed May 6, 2024, https://www.bcponline.org/General/nicene_creed.html.

CHAPTER 5

1. Charles F. Stanley, *Handle With Prayer* (Colorado Springs, CO: David C Cook, 2011), 11, https://www.amazon.com/Handle-Prayer-Unwrap-Source-Strength/dp/1434709442?.
2. F. B. Meyer, quoted in Jerry Sittser, *When God Doesn't Answer Your Prayer* (Grand Rapids, MI: Zondervan, 2007), 19, https://www.google.com/books/edition/When_God_Doesn_t_Answer_Your_Prayer/WL2ldRdKwMkC?hl=en&gbpv=0.
3. *Rocky V*, directed by John G. Avildsen (Star Partners III, Ltd. and Chartoff-Winkler Productions, 1990).
4. William Cowper, *Memoir of the Early Life of William Cowper, Esq.* (London: R. Edwards, 1816), 29–43, https://wellcomecollection.org/works/u8qp6p8z.

5. Cowper, *Memoir of the Early Life of William Cowper*, 67–68.
6. William Cowper, "Hymn 60: Exhortation to Prayer," Olney Hymns, 1779, https://www.ccel.org/ccel/n/newton/olneyhymns/cache/olneyhymns.pdf.
7. "Center for Spiritual Growth," St. David's Episcopal Church, accessed May 6, 2024, https://stdavidschurch.org/adult-formation/center-for-spiritual-growth/.
8. William Cowper, "There Is a Fountain Filled with Blood," 1772, https://hymnary.org/text/there_is_a_fountain_filled_with_blood_dr.

Chapter 6

1. Adrian Rogers, "It Is Decision That Determines Destiny," Love Worth Finding, 2022, https://www.lwf.org/pdfs/2086-It-Is-Decision-That-Determines-Destiny-PTR.pdf.
2. C. S. Lewis, *A Grief Observed* (New York: HarperCollins, 1996), 6, https://www.amazon.com/Grief-Observed-C-S-Lewis/dp/0060652381.
3. Lewis, *A Grief Observed*, 6–7.
4. Lewis, *A Grief Observed*, 65.
5. Charles Morris, "A Closer Look at 'Checkmate,'" Haven Today, February 22, 2021, https://haventoday.org/blog/closer-look-checkmate/.

Chapter 8

1. Inner Circle is a community of people relentlessly pursuing all that God has for them. Join the Inner Circle for spiritual warfare to be equipped in the battlefields of your spiritual life and to know how to take down the enemy, his kingdom, and his demonic attacks, in Jesus' mighty name. You can join today at https://johnramirez.org/inner-circle/.

Chapter 10

1. Wikipedia, s.v. "Hope (Watts)," last edited March 22, 2024, https://en.wikipedia.org/wiki/Hope_(Watts).
2. Jacob Gijy, "'Breaking My Goggles on Purpose'—Michael Phelps' Coach Used a Harsh Training Technique to Prepare Him for the Challenges," Essentially Sports, May 30, 2022, https://www.essentiallysports.com/

us-sports-news-swimming-news-breaking-my-goggles-on-purpose-michael-phelps-coach-used-a-harsh-training-technique-to-prepare-him-for-the-challenges/.

3. Ira Deokule, "'My goggles fill up with water...I counted my strokes'—Michael Phelps on how he swam 'blind' at the 2008 Olympics," Sportskeeda, modified March 13, 2024, https://www.sportskeeda.com/us/olympics/michael-phelps-swam-blind-2008-olympics.

CHAPTER 11

1. Martin Luther, Table Talk, cccc, Christian Classics Ethereal Library, accessed May 6, 2024, https://www.ccel.org/ccel/luther/tabletalk.v.xvii.html.
2. Fulton J. Sheen, "A Plea for Intolerance," Roman Catholic Man, April 24, 2023, https://romancatholicman.com/wp/a-plea-for-intolerance-by-venerable-fulton-j-sheen-2/.
3. Quoted in Dennis Phelps, "What Can Preachers Learn from Billy Graham?" Preaching.com, accessed May 6, 2024, https://www.preaching.com/articles/what-can-preachers-learn-from-billy-graham/.
4. R. C. Sproul, "Healing of the Man with the Unclean Spirit," December 4, 2005, https://www.ligonier.org/learn/sermons/mark-healing-man-unclean.

CHAPTER 12

1. A. W. Tozer, *The Root of the Righteous* (Chicago: Moody Publishers, 1986), 189, https://www.amazon.com/Root-Righteous-W-Tozer/dp/160066797X?.
2. Tozer, *The Root of the Righteous*, 189.
3. Office of Communications & Public Engagement, "Josh McDowell tells his personal story of forgiveness," Liberty University, February 5, 2014, https://www.liberty.edu/news/2014/02/05/josh-mcdowell-tells-his-personal-story-of-forgiveness/.
4. Charles Haddon Spurgeon, "The Church the World's Hope," March 1, 1863, Metropolitan Tabernacle, https://www.spurgeon.org/resource-library/sermons/the-church-the-worlds-hope/#flipbook/.
5. A. W. Tozer, *That Incredible Christian* (Harrisburg, PA: Christian Publications, 1964), 82, https://archive.org/details/thatincrediblech00awto/page/n5/mode/2up.

CHAPTER 13

1. J. C. Ryle, *Expository Thoughts on the Gospels*, Monergism, accessed May 16, 2024, https://www.monergism.com/thethreshold/sdg/expository_web.html.
2. Ryle, *Expository Thoughts on the Gospels*.
3. Derek W. H. Thomas, *What Is Providence?* (Phillipsburg, NJ: P & R Publishing, 2008), 33, https://archive.org/details/whatisprovidence0000thom.
4. Duncan Campbell, "Address on Revival," oChristian.com, accessed May 16, 2024, http://articles.ochristian.com/article10394.shtml.

Contact John Ramirez Ministries at
info@johnramirez.org

My FREE GIFT to You

Dear Reader,

The devil works hard, but God works harder! By finishing my book, I am proud to say that you have gained the invaluable tools needed to fight in the spirit and take up your God-given authority as more than a conqueror in Christ Jesus.

To show my gratitude, I am offering the eBook, *Fire Prayers*, for **FREE!**

To secure your **FREE GIFT**, please go to **MyCharismaShop. com/pages/exposing2024.**

Rejoice in the Lord,

Scan to get your FREE eBook!

CHARISMA
HOUSE